HE
HER HONOUR
&
SHE
HIS GLORY

Other books by Vernon S. Grieger

Earthly Images of the Heavenly Bride:
Women and the Church

Sanctify Us through Thy Truth
Selected Sermons Vol. 1

The Word Shall Stand:
Our Evangelical Lutheran Confession
by M.J.Grieger, V.S.Grieger, C.R. Priebbenow

Other books by Vernon S. Grieger

Earthly Images of the Heavenly Bride:
Women and the Church

Sanctify Us through Thy Truth
Selected Sermons Vols. 1, 2, 3, and 4

The Word Shall Stand:
Our Evangelical Lutheran Confession
by M.J.Grieger, V.S.Grieger, C.R. Priebbenow

He
Her Honour
&
She
His Glory

By V.S. Grieger

Published and Copyright by the author April 1994
17 Edmond St. Marburg, Queensland 4346
1st edition limited 40 copies April 1994
2nd edition revised April 1994
3rd edition revised September 1994
4th edition May 2001
5th edition April 2008

National Library of Australia
Cataloguing-in-Publication entry

   Grieger, Vernon S.
      He, her honour & she, his glory.
      ISBN 978-0-646-18375-6.
      1. Marriage - Religious aspects - Christianity. 2. Married
      people - Religious life. I. Title II. Title : He, her honour
      and she, his glory.

241.63

Slightly revised edition October 2014

ACKNOWLEDGMENTS
The author wishes to express his deep thanks and appreciation
for those who helped in the preparation of this book, by reading it
critically and making helpful suggestions. Special thanks is due
to Susan Robertson, of Luther Rose Publications, whose expertise
and tireless efforts helped to express the principles outlined here.
Her understanding, insights and numerous corrections have con-
tributed immensely to the readability of this book.

Scripture quotations that appear unidentified throughout the
book are from the King James Version of the Bible.
Scripture quotations identified RAV are from the Revised Autho-
rised Version. Copyright 1982.
Scripture quotations identified as RSV are from the Revised Stan-
dard Version of the Bible. Copyrighted 1946 and 1952.
Published by Lutheran News
Printed by Lightning Source, Inc., La Vergne, TN

DEDICATION

This book is dedicated to the memory of my most precious wife, Joyce, whom I committed into the arms of our loving heavenly Bridegroom just two years prior to the date of publication. From her I learned to understand at least something of the most amazing and wonderful nature of woman. Together we were privileged to enjoy something of the honour and glory that God intended for man and woman in marriage. This leads me to give thanks to God and to pray that our children and many others will be able to share this same joy in a confused and misguided world.

V.S.Grieger

A Bridegroom's Prayer

That I may come near to her,
draw me nearer to you than to her;
that I may know her,
make me to know you more than her;
that I may love her
with the love of a perfectly whole heart, cause me to love
you more than her and most of all.

Temple Gairdner
1873-1928

CONTENTS

DIAGRAMS

PREFACE

Every young couple surely wants to make theirs the most happy and rewarding marriage, but they are often disturbed by two fears. First they are surrounded by friends and acquaintances who seem to be such sensible and decent people and yet they are distressed by matrimonial failure and broken hearts. Their marriage is a disaster and may end in divorce. Does this mean that there are unknown forces which could also wreck their marriage? Another misgiving arises from the fact that it seems to be generally assumed that even a very good marriage may begin with great affection and devotion between partners, but then, with the passing of time, perhaps a year or two, they become less affectionate and begin simply to take each other for granted. Love dissolves into loyalty, and they are left simply to sharing the same house as they get on with the job of making a living, without any real affection and endearment toward each other. If a wife should be seen sitting close to her husband in their car it is at once assumed that they must be only very recently married. Mature married couples just don't act that way. Is this the way it really ought to be?

To any young couple deeply in love, it seems as if most of the joy and sizzle has gone out of such a marriage, and they would not like this to happen to them. Is this really an evidence of a good marriage? Shouldn't it be the other way around, that the love and affection of a couple for each other actually grows stronger and more expressive with the passing of time, so that after twenty five years of marriage they should be much more deeply affectionate and devoted to each other than they were on their honeymoon? This would seem to them to be not only more natural but more desirable. Isn't it possible for them to have a marriage relationship in which their devotion for each other grows stronger and deeper with the passing of time? How can this be achieved? They know instinctively that marriage should provide the highest fulfilment for man and woman in life, but they don't want to have to experiment with various matrimonial possibilities, to find out, by trial and error, which principles are sound, and which are disruptive of a happy marriage.

It is the aim of this book to point to sound, biblical principles by which Christian couples can not only make theirs a wonderful and rewarding marriage, but one which will become even more wonderful and glorious with experience and the passing of time. In doing so, no other guide will be used, and no other authority recognised, than that of the Author of marriage himself, as revealed in his Word – the Holy Scriptures. Academic scholars may look in vain for an imposing bibliography of psychological, sociological, anthropological, or theological works. The principles herein advocated are derived from only one source – the holy Scriptures – reinforced by practical experience. It is the author's conviction that if these are properly understood by intelligent and humble Christians, little else is necessary.

Readers who are not Christians may be inclined to object to seeking directions from the Bible. This is understandable. This writer would not regard the sacred writings of various eastern religions as having any authority for him. But that would not prevent him from considering the validity of their claims, especially with regard to such an important matter as marriage. While many academics are often more concerned with the question of *who* is saying something, than *what* is being said, the question that must ultimately be faced is whether or not the principles, or the model of marriage, as set forth in the Bible, is in fact true. Is it good or not? Does it portray a relationship that is truly satisfying and in the best interests of men and women? Does it uplift and refine people so that society is improved by it? Or is it degrading? It is the writer's conviction that the relationship between men and women, especially in marriage, as it is portrayed and taught in the Bible, would be almost universally accepted as best for mankind if people truly understood it; not simply because it comes from the Bible, but because it is a true description of what is both natural and necessary for men and women. Unless people are trained in, or given to some false, unnatural ideology, they would almost surely be happy with, and delighted to live out what the Bible prescribes, simply because they would find it uplifting and fulfilling in the deepest sense of those words.

This book does not deal with physical and sexual relationships, except to say that exactly the same principles must apply there as in other areas of married life. It must be governed by a self-sacrificing love on the part of the husband, and a self-surrendering love on the part of the wife. The reason for omitting a study of this matter is not because it is considered relatively unimportant. On the contrary, the sexual relationship of husband and wife is extremely important. For the Christian it is, or at least ought to be, a unique celebration of the relationship between Christ and his Church. It is a portrayal of the mysterious, almost unbelievable union between Christ and his Church – something truly sacred and glorious for which a Christian couple will give thanks and praise to God, and will enjoy to his honour and glory.

Chapter 1

THE STONES CRY OUT

Marriage and the family were intended to be the most precious and sacred institutions that men and women can enjoy here in this world. They have been the most popular topic of the dreams, the fancies and longings, the songs and poetry, the plays and movies, the music and fantasy of the human race throughout history. The relationship between man and woman is fundamentally more important to people, civilised or not, than all the wars and political struggles that the world has seen. Ultimately it is more important and of greater consequence, than any ideology or system of government. It is better and more satisfying for a man to live harmoniously with his wife and family under a totalitarian regime, than to live in a frustrated, bickering marriage and family in a free and democratic country. The most deplorable devastation of wars is terrible, not so much because of the ruthless destruction of houses and cities, beautiful buildings, and important services, but because of the ruin of the lives of men and women, and their families. These are the wounds that bleed the longest and cause the deepest pain, because they cut right down into that which is most vital and precious in life – that which truly makes life worth living.

The fact that many marriages and families are anything but glorious and enjoyable, is due, not to an inherent weakness or defect in the institution of marriage itself, but to a degenerate imitation of it, or to an abuse of it at the hands of immature players, and possibly professional innovators who have never understood the true nature of this institution. Even though the world may not understand what this relationship should be, and how it should be regulated, yet it generally has a gut-feeling that this is something very important – something that should be the source of the most wonderful joy and happiness in life.

And yet today there is virtually no agreement as to the nature of life between the sexes, and by what principles it should be guided. Some cry one thing and others another. Some insist on equality and interchange ability, others contend for different roles and responsibilities between men and women. Some demand a fifty/fifty democratic sharing of responsibility and authority, others see marriage rather as a king/queen, or sovereign relationship. Some contend for a loose, temporary relationship in marriage that may be dissolved by mutual agreement, and others assert that it must be for life. Some insist on as much independence between

1

partners as possible, while others would strive for complete inter-dependence. Some go so far as to argue that marriage should be abolished and that men and women should be free to make and abandon relationships as their emotions direct them, while others hold that only the closest and most permanent relationship in marriage will provide true joy and happiness, and real stability in the community.

With all this confusion and disagreement, not only among the amateurs and laymen, but especially among the professional, social workers and marriage guidance counsellors, how can there be any help or clear direction? After so many years of debate, how can anyone still make a meaningful contribution? How can anyone claim to speak with authority, and infer that what he believes is true, when that will immediately be questioned and rejected by a myriad of learned experts and academic social planners who are arguing among themselves? This situation has led many to be utterly sceptical and even to contend for the complete abolition of marriage, in favour of some new social system devised to "meet our modern needs" more adequately.

One would expect that this matter should have been the subject of the most in-depth and intense study by the really great, learned and wise men and women of the world. When this is done one would hope that they might instruct us and see to it that marriage and the family are not only protected and preserved among us, but strengthened, exulted, and glorified in society. But when these hold their peace, there comes a time when even the wretched stones must begin to cry out.[1] This book is the voice of one such rough, uncut and unpolished stone.

Hopefully it may move others, in our generation, to cut down a few branches from the trees or to spread their clothes in the way,[2] so as to honour what seems to the world as nothing but an ass's burden, but which is really a most precious gift of God to his people, and which has the potential to bestow on them the greatest joy and happiness that is possible for us here in this world.

There are two reasons why the writer dares to express what he believes on this matter. The first is, that he believes that what he is about to say is not his own ideas or theories, but is ultimately the teaching and direction of him who is the true Author and Creator of marriage, and who knows both what that relationship should be, and how it will bring the most joy and happiness to man and woman. This has been learned both from some study of the Word and truth of the Author of marriage, and from personal

---

[1] cp. Luke 19:40

[2] cp. Matt. 21:8

experience in trying to put these principles into practice.

The second reason is a simple belief that when all the learned arguments have been presented, when all the experts have sounded forth and unloaded their knowledge, and the radical agitators have ceased their shrieking and revolutionary demands, when all the chips are down and the dust has finally settled, there will be left a certain, unsophisticated simplicity in the heart of ordinary men and women which will move a noble young man to take his bride into his arms and say to her from the depth of his heart, "I Joe Blo take you, Mary Jones to be my wedded wife. I promise and vow to be true to you, to love you and keep you, in sickness and in health, in prosperity and adversity, so long as we both shall live." And she will say in reply, "I, Mary Jones, take you, Joe Blo to be my wedded husband. I promise and vow to be true to you, to love and obey you, to cherish and honour you in sickness and in health, in prosperity and in adversity, so long as we both shall live." And no matter who is looking, they will seal this vow with lips that not only speak words of reason but also reveal convictions against which nobody can argue.

Hans Christian Andersen long ago pointed to the power of this innocent, but disarming simplicity in his tale of the emperor's new clothes. Because certain swindlers had asserted that the expensive cloth, of which they pretended to be making a new suit for the emperor, was absolutely invisible to a fool, and because nobody wanted to appear a fool, everybody pretended to see and admire the beauty of the non-existent suit, and joined in singing the praises of this creation, until a little boy, in his innocence, unaware of the shame of being exposed as a fool, dared to cry out that the king was parading in the nude. Sometimes the plain truth is more obvious to simple people than to sophisticated experts,[3] who are very conscious of the pressure of modern trends and popular opinion.

When the biblical principles have been clearly outlined and understood, there will be, even in the most sophisticated of people, a deep-down conviction that this is the way it truly ought to be, despite all the propaganda to the contrary. This is really what men and women need and want. These are eternal truths that neither alter with time nor go out of fashion with changing conditions. Though marriage was instituted in the Garden of Eden,[4] men and women are still basically the same today as they were then, and their needs in this area remain the same, whether or not they are Christians, and whether or not they want to be guided by the teachings of the Bible.

---

[3] Matt. 11:25
[4] cp. Gen. 2:18-25

3

Chapter 2

MAN AND WOMAN
DESIGNED TO BE DIFFERENT

The first and most basic question that we must face is whether there is or ought to be any difference between men and women, other than in their purely reproductive processes. That there are great differences between the sexes with regard to virtually everything in life, has been accepted for thousands of years, throughout the history of the human race.

It has been the dubious distinction of our present generation, on the other hand, to question, and indeed seriously to deny, what was more than obvious even to the children of virtually every tribe and race of civilised mankind in history. It seems a pity to have to spend time asserting what is so clear and should never have been questioned by rational beings, and yet this appears to be necessary because it is seriously contended today that the difference between male and female, apart from their reproductive functions, is only the result of conditioning from childhood on. It is claimed that our poor, unfortunate, little girls finish up with feminine ways and habits because their sexist mothers put dresses on them, and give them dolls to play with. Similarly it is because our little boys are given cars and bulldozers and guns to play with, that they develop what are now called masculine traits. If our little girls were given tractors and guns instead, and our little boys were given dolls and pretty dresses, their ways and habits would be reversed. All of their character and personality is the result of environmental influences, not of any innate or instinctive masculine or feminine character.

This is a theory that can be believed only because of constant repetition, brain-washing, or because of wishful thinking and ideological prejudice. There is no scientific data and no experience to back it up; nor has there ever been any. One wonders whether it could ever seriously be asserted by any who have had the joy of rearing their own children. But, of course, it is the necessary foundation of much popular, modern thinking and belief. Unless it is true that there are no innate differences between men and women, psychologically and emotionally, as well as physically, it would have to be conceded that there ought to be different roles and functions for men and women. If they are really different, men might conceivably be better at some things than women, and women might be better at other things than men. In this case it

4

would be foolish and unrealistic to demand absolute equality and interchange ability between them. Discrimination on the basis of sex would have some legitimate basis. The whole philosophy could crumble and become unbelievable. And so it must continue to be asserted loudly and clearly that there are no essential, innate differences between men and women, no matter what experience shows.

People who don't trust their own or even the universal experience of mankind, are blind leaders, and can not expect others to trust their assertions which are contrary to common experience. We can only wish them the sobering joy of watching their own little girls, without any prompting or parental guidance, dressing up and playing at weddings, while their little boys look on with disinterest, or run off to do something they think is not so sissy. And we would plead with them, before they set about to punish and eradicate such "sexist" behaviour of children to ask themselves whether it isn't really something beautiful that they would do well to encourage rather than condemn.

Not only has universal experience shown that sexual differences between boys and girls, show up in almost every facet of life, but this has been conclusively demonstrated and proven by scientific experiment. Unless we want to take our stand with the flat earth people, it is simply too late in history to make the claim that there are no sexual differences between male and female, other than in the reproductive realm. This has been disproved too often and too consistently in the last 20 years to have any semblance of validity whatever. For anyone not able to, or not interested in reading up a multitude of scientific articles on the subject, Anne Moir and David Jessel, in their book *Brainsex: the real difference between men & women,*[5] show that it is the universal conclusion of numerous scientific experiments conducted in very recent years, not only that there are numerous differences between men and women, physical as well as psychological, but that these differences have their origin in biology and hormonal influences, so that they are determined for the most part long before birth. They have shown, in fact, that the most distinctive organ differentiating men and women, is not in the reproductive group at all, but is the brain. And since the brain controls virtually everything else, the differences between men and women will be obvious in virtually everything they think, say or do. These are not only hard scientific facts, but they are backed up by the universal experience of all history.

[5] *Brainsex* by Anne Moir and David Jessel, Mandarin, 1991

The Bible clearly teaches that men and women are different, and have different roles in relation to each other, not regulated by prevailing custom or conditions of the times but based upon one unchangeable event – the creation of man and woman in the very beginning. They are different and act differently simply because they were made to be different.[6] Even the Fall into sin, while it, to some extent, affected the relationship between man and woman, is never seen as the basis for the differences between them or their different roles in life. Nor has the work of redemption removed these differences in their natures and roles.

The notion that Christ, by the redemption, somehow did away with all differences between man and woman, is denied by the very passage which people clutch at to support such a view. Paul says in Galatians 3:27-28, *"For as many of you as have been baptised into Christ have put on Christ. There is neither Jew nor Greek, there is neither bond nor free, there is neither male nor female: for ye are all one in Christ Jesus."* Not only is it quite clear that the apostle is speaking of our spiritual relationship to each other in Christ, and not of our relationship here in this physical world, where these relationships continue, as he teaches elsewhere,[7] but he goes on at once to assert, *"And if ye be Christ's, then are ye Abraham's seed, and heirs according to the promise."* (Galatians 3:29). The relationship that believers have in Christ makes them Abraham's seed and heirs. But Abraham's seed and heirs had a very marked distinction between male and female in their earthly functions. It was Abraham's seed that had the special covenant of circumcision. Of course, only males were to be circumcised and could officiate as priests in the temple, and so on. And yet all Israel, male and female, were equally covered by the covenant relationship with God. So the Christians too, in their relationship with Christ are neither male nor female, but, as Abraham's seed, in their earthly functions they will always continue to be male and female. In fact these differences are part of their glory, as we shall see later.

How were the differences between man and woman built into them at their creation? The passage that most significantly highlights the differences between man and woman in creation is the account of the creation of woman in Genesis 2:18-25. *"And the Lord God said, It is not good that man should be alone; I will make him an help meet for him. And out of the ground the Lord God formed every beast of the field, and every fowl of the air; and brought them unto Adam to see what he would call them: and*

---

[6] cp. I Cor. 11:13-16; Eph 5:31-32; I Tim. 2:11-14

[7] cp. II Tim. 2:11-15 etc.

whatsoever Adam called every living creature, that was the name thereof. And Adam gave names to all cattle, and to the fowl of the air, and to every beast of the field; but for Adam there was not found an help meet for him. And the Lord God caused a deep sleep to fall upon Adam, and he slept: and he took one of his ribs, and closed up the flesh instead thereof; and the rib, which the Lord God had taken from man, made he a woman, and brought her unto the man. And Adam said, This is now bone of my bones, and flesh of my flesh: she shall be called Woman, because she was taken out of Man. Therefore shall a man leave his father and his mother, and shall cleave unto his wife: and they shall be one flesh. And they were both naked, the man and his wife, and were not ashamed."

We might wonder why it was that God did it like this. Why didn't he make both Adam and Eve together at the same time? Surely he knew before he created man that it wouldn't be any good for him to be alone. He didn't create Adam alone first to see how he would go, and then found out by experience that it was just no good that way, and so he had to set about to create a partner for him. No, God knew all the time that this would not be any good, but he no doubt had a purpose in creating Adam first, and allowing him to be alone for a time. It was probably to impress upon him and us that it is just no good for man to be alone, so that man will not simply take woman for granted, but come to realise that she is of tremendous importance for him. He is no good without her.

But why wasn't it good for Adam to be alone? He was created perfect in every respect − a most wonderful creature. In the perfection of the Garden of Eden he did not need anyone to cook or sew, or wash and iron his clothes. He had plenty to eat and drink. Everything was laid on, as it were. He could simply eat of the abundant fruits all around him. The climate was ideal so that there was no need for clothing to keep warm. Everything was perfect for him. And so, on the face of it, it might well have seemed that Adam especially had no need for woman. He could have lived happily by himself for thousands of years.

But perhaps someone will say that Adam probably needed other human company, in the sense of someone to talk to and share his experiences. If that was what Adam needed God would no doubt have made another man or several men as companions for him. Men can usually talk far more freely among themselves and share their experiences better with men than with women. In fact many men are embarrassed and somewhat shy in the company of women. If Adam simply needed company, he could have had the company of other men. It must have been something else that was not good about man being alone, otherwise why should God have made a woman for man?

The answer to this lies in God's words, *"I will make him an help meet for him."* What is a helpmeet? Unfortunately this English term *"helpmeet"* gives a completely wrong impression. It suggests someone to help man in the sense of cooking his meals, sewing and washing his clothes for him and so on. But Adam did not need anything like that. No, the original Hebrew words for *"help meet"* are EZER K'NEGEDO which really means a helper who is like him but opposite to him − that is a complementary counterpart. Man, as he was created, required someone to supply what he lacked in order to make him complete. That is why it was not good that man should be alone. He had an inherent lack or need that could be fulfilled only by another special creation − the creation of woman from his own flesh and bone. That was the purpose of God in creating a woman for him. He needed a complement. A man could never have supplied this.

This is a very important truth that our modern society needs to re-learn. Most people seem to assume that both men and women are complete in themselves so that they can live as independent individuals more or less in competition with each other. The only differences between them are sexual for the sake of procreation. Men and women are considered to be basically identical in all but a few biological features. They are thought to have the same abilities and the same interests, so that they are virtually interchangeable. But this is not what the Lord made when he made Eve for Adam. She was to be something quite different from him − someone to supply what he lacked so that they together might be complete.

Incidentally it is surely this truth that brings the greatest honour and glory to woman. If she were simply, or almost exactly like man, except for certain reproductive functions, then she would be nothing special at all. But it is in her unique character − her difference from man − that her true worth and glory lie. Without her, man is not good. His whole worth and welfare are bound up with, and dependent upon, her unique nature. The more we appreciate woman's differences from man, the more important she becomes to us. This is why the present anti-discrimination or unisex philosophy is so dangerous. While those who advocate this may think they are aiding the image and appreciation of women, they are in fact doing the very opposite. They are robbing woman of her unique worth and true glory in society, her very reason for existence. As a result she becomes a "nothing special" that man could virtually do without − hardly worth noticing! This is probably the meanest treatment that man can possibly give to woman, especially to his wife. He might disappoint her in many ways; he might fail to do for her what he ought; he might be remiss in supplying her needs, but he dare not fail to notice her and treat her as if she were nothing special. This is to strike at the very heart of woman. It robs her of all meaning and purpose. She is what she is only because she is different from man – wonderfully different, and importantly different. And if that difference is not seen or recognised as important she might as well disappear.

This is the cause of so much disappointment, frustration, loss of personal worth and self-esteem in women today, not to mention depression which seems to be on the increase. Unless her differences are appreciated and treasured she is robbed of her very reason for being, and man in his folly might as well live alone – the very thing that God said was not good in the first place. Ultimately, then, the assertion that woman is virtually the same as man, and is to be treated like man, is the most radical attack upon her dignity and worth. It is not discrimination between man and woman that is the really great evil, but a failure to discriminate or differentiate between them, that is the most dangerous threat. It has been pointed out that all "liberation" movements have a habit of leading to the slavery of the very ones they profess to be liberating, and that the Women's Liberation movement will be no exception as long as it persists in its present course.

We need to realise that the Hebrew expression EZER K'-NEGEDO (help meet) indicates not only that woman was to be different from man, in the sense of being complementary, so that she supplied what he lacked, but also that her differences from man would be such that she would be his counterpart or opposite in many respects. In other words the relationship between man and woman was to be such that, not only would she supply those vital human qualities that he lacked, while he would have important qualities that she lacked – where he was stronger she would be weaker, and where he was weaker she would be stronger, each complementing the other – but also her qualities would be opposite to his. While man was outgoing and aggressive by nature, woman would be reserved and receptive. In this way man with his masculine qualities, his physical strength, initiative, leadership and determination, and woman with her different, feminine qualities and capabilities, her beauty, grace, charm and delicate interest in the finer things of life, would beautifully complement each other. The two of them together were necessary to make up one complete and well-balanced human unit.

This relationship would be most necessary and find its fullest expression within marriage, where man and woman were to be one flesh, but it would also be very important within society generally, where men, if they are properly masculine, and women, if they are truly feminine, each have distinctive contributions to make for the well being of the community. Virtually everything about men and women, even their voices, is designed to be complementary, so that where this is properly recognised and appreciated, they can live in the most wonderful harmony.

From this it should be evident that there is a radical difference between the way modern humanism or feminism sees the relationship between man and woman, and the way it is outlined in the Scriptures. The Bible sees man and woman as complementary counterparts of each other, different and opposite in many respects. Because each one supplies those human qualities that the other lacks, they have different roles in life, and the two together are necessary for a proper balanced society. The humanist view, by contrast, is that man and woman are simply two individuals, almost the same and virtually interchangeable. They are equal competitors in the game of life.

The Christian sees marriage as a lifelong union of two people to form a mutually dependent unit, so that they are no longer two but one flesh. They each have different roles and responsibilities, the husband being the head of the wife, and the wife being the glory of her husband. Humanist philosophy, on the other hand, sees marriage as nothing more than a contract between two independent individuals working together and living together for mutual benefit. Each partner remains an independent individual in this contract, sharing their authority, their rights and responsibilities on a more or less fifty/fifty basis.

The biblical view sees men and women as gloriously different. It treasures masculinity and femininity, appreciating men for their masculine qualities and contribution to society, and appreciating women for their remarkable, feminine qualities and contribution to society. It is the differences between them that are truly wonderful and important. Unisex philosophy, on the other hand, not only demands interchangeable rights and responsibilities for men and women, but seeks to erase and to deny the worth of the differences between men and women. This relationship between men and women is illustrated diagrammatically at the back of this book. These diagrams are adapted from my book *Earthly Images of the Heavenly Bride: Women and the Church*, Luther Rose Publications, 1992.

If we accept the scriptural account of the creation of man and woman as a true and historical fact, then at least the following is clear. God created man and woman separately and at different times. He created them from different material and in a different way, man from the dust of the ground, and woman from the already genetically coded flesh and bone of Adam. Since it was not good for man to be alone, he created woman to complement him, so that the two together would be one complete and well-balanced unit. This has got to mean that man and woman are different and are to have different roles and functions in life.

This is not only the clear teaching of Scripture, but it is demonstrated by overwhelming, scientific experimentation and proof. It is finally one of the most obvious truths in nature, that can be denied only by a misguided and wilfully blind ideology. And the double tragedy is that such denial, not only flies in the face of all evidence, but that it is thought to be in the interest of women and their status in society, when in fact it is the death blow to their dignity and worth. If carried through to its logical conclusions, this deception has the potential to undermine all respect for women and their unique worth in society.

But is the biblical view of the relationship between man and woman really conducive to harmony between the sexes, and to a healthy, respect and high regard for women? Isn't it really because Judeo/Christian society has followed this biblical pattern for so long, that women have suffered so many insults and been so deprived in society? It is the contention of the author that the very opposite is true. Because society has not understood the biblical principles, and has failed to follow them, the relationship between men and women has not been what it should, and women have suffered as a result. This has not been the fault of society only, but of the church too, whose business it was to expound upon and promote the principles of Scripture. The churches have been remiss in this – seriously remiss. Following the popular trends of the time they have largely failed either to understand or to apply the truths of God's Word in this matter. It will therefore be the aim of the following pages to seek to understand, and to apply what Scripture sees as the proper relationship between man and woman.

Chapter 3

AUTHORITY
AND THE PARADOXICAL POWER OF
TRUE FEMININITY

While the Bible speaks of rulers exercising authority over their subjects, and requires us all to submit to those in authority,[8] it at the same time insists that all such power and authority, exercised by man, is from God. He alone has all power in heaven and on earth, as Jesus reminds us.[9] This can only mean that any power exercised by manby parents over children, or rulers over subjects, does not belong essentially to man himself, but to God. Man can only exercise God's power and authority as his deputy. St. Paul makes this quite clear in the words, *"The powers that be are ordained of God, whosoever therefore resisteth the power, resisteth the ordinance of God: and they that resist shall receive unto themselves damnation."* (Romans 13:1-2). Clearly we must obey those in authority over us as we would obey God himself.

From this it should be evident that when God ordained that the husband is to be the head of the wife, and that she is to be subject to him, this does not imply that he has any power or authority of his own, on account of which his wife is to be subject to him. That is impossible since Christ himself has all power in heaven and on earth. The reason why the wife is to be subject to him, as unto the Lord, is because God has ordained it that the husband is to exercise the authority of God in their relationship and in their family. He is God's representative to see to it that God's will is done, and it is he who must give a final account to God for the way this function has been carried out. The reason why the wife is to be subject to her husband, as to the Lord, then, is simply because it is his onerous responsibility to exercise the authority of God in their relationship. It is a question of God's order, not a matter of superiority or personal power.

In I Corinthians 11:3, St. Paul says, *"I would have you know, that the head of every man is Christ; and the head of the woman is the man; and the head of Christ is God."* The line of authority or responsibility in God's order is, GOD CHRIST MAN WOMAN. This is not a human arrangement invented by some primitive, male-dominated society, and forced on generations of victims. It

---

[8] cp. Rom. 13:1-5; 1 Pet. 2:18.

[9] cp. Matt. 28:18.

is the ordinance of God himself, and something that will continue to exist whether man recognises it or not. Just as parents can not agree to hand over their God-given authority to their children, so man can not abdicate this authority either. He will finally have to give an account to God for the way in which he administered it.

The power and authority referred to here is what might be called a positive or active power in distinction from a negative or passive force. Positive power consists of all kinds of physical force, mechanical energy and leverage, military might, political authority, and the power of numbers or overwhelming majority and strength. It is the ability to control others or make them do as you want in a positive way. This is the only sort of power that most people know or recognise. But there is another power of quite a different nature, which operates in the very opposite way — a sort of negative or passive force.

The Bible speaks of this peculiar power as a strength that is made perfect in weakness. When St. Paul asked the Lord to take away his thorn in the flesh, the Lord said to him, *"My grace is sufficient for thee: for my strength is made perfect in weakness."* And St. Paul adds in the next verse, *"When I am weak, then am I strong."* (II Corinthians 12:9-10). This may sound like a contradiction to many. It is certainly a paradox, but it is nevertheless a fact. This kind of negative force is a mystery to most people, and yet it is of tremendous importance and effect.

There are notable examples of both kinds of power in our Lord Jesus Christ. As the Son of God, Jesus had all power in heaven and earth, both active and passive. He used his active power in the creation of the mighty universe so that, as John says, *"All things were made by him; and without him was not anything made that was made"* (John 1:3). To do this would have required power which is beyond our imagination. He also has the power to destroy this world again, and will finally do so at the end of time.[10] Even in his humiliation Jesus had the authority to perform mighty miracles. At his word the sick were made well, water turned to wine, the raging sea was quieted, and the dead came back to life. Even as he was about to be arrested in the Garden of Gethsemane, one word from him caused his enemies to fall to the ground.[11]

But he also had great passive power — a strength that was made perfect in weakness. When he was threatened by his enemies, so that it seemed that his great, almighty power would have been most necessary, Jesus absolutely refused to use it, but meekly submitted himself to the abuse of his enemies. He allowed himself to be arrested, to be tried illegally before the Jewish court,

[10] cp. II Pet. 3:10

[11] cp. John 18:5f.

13

and to be crucified on Calvary. Even as he hung there upon the cross, there was another challenge for him to use his almighty power, as the Son of God, and save himself. The chief priests and elders of the people said, *"If he be the King of Israel, let him now come down from the cross, and we will believe him. He trusted in God; let him deliver him now, if he will have him: for he said, I am the Son of God."* (Matthew 27:42f.). One would have thought that that would have been a great opportunity for Jesus to display his almighty power and come down from the cross to show his enemies that he was indeed the Son of God with all authority, so that even the leaders of the Jews would have been obliged to believe in him, as they conceded. Instead he meekly submitted to their insults and finally bowed his head in death. It seemed to everyone as if he had gone down in weakness and utter defeat. But what was the final outcome? It was just by his suffering and death that he won the victory, not only over his enemies among the Jews, but over Satan and all his legions as well. The greatest victory that this world has ever seen was accomplished not by physical force and power, but by humble submission – by a strength that is made perfect in weakness. This is why the Gospel of a crucified Christ seems so foolish to the power-hungry world. It is a stumbling block to the Jews and foolishness to the Greeks, but really it is *"the power of God and the wisdom of God."* (I Corinthians 1:24). It is the power by which God establishes his Church.

This strength is not limited only to Christ, but it is available also to Christians. In fact this was the power by which St. Paul carried out his great mission to the world. When he was attacked, and persecuted, by his enemies, forcefully thrown out of synagogues, dragged out of the city and stoned at Lystra,[12] he never once resorted to physical force in order to protect himself or defend himself against his enemies. He simply submitted to all their abuse. And what was the final result? Clearly he won the victory over all his foes. His cause was triumphant. The Gospel flourished and Christ was proclaimed in all of Asia, as his enemies too had to acknowledge.[13]

This same power is exercised by Christians still today. All the work of the Church – its mission to the world is to be carried out not by that active physical force. The Church will never convert anyone to Christ with the use of positive power, threats and physical force. Whenever in history the church resorted to the use of such power, it did so to its own shame and harm. Such power has

---

[12] cp. Acts 14:19
[13] cp. Acts 19:10

not been given to the Church. As the Bride of Christ she can use only what St. Paul used in his work – the strength that is made perfect in weakness. And with that she can conquer formidable foes.

How did it happen that the Christian Church survived in China? Before the atheistic communists took over that country there were some 835,000 Christians there. The atheistic government began a systematic persecution of the Christian Church in order to destroy it utterly. Worship services were forbidden, Bibles and Christian literature were confiscated and burned. A person could be put to death for having so much as one page of the Bible in his possession. Christians were forbidden to teach their children the way of salvation, and were punished severely and imprisoned for any failure to comply. Christians were put out of work, imprisoned, tortured and put to death, often in the most brutal and unmentionable ways. From a worldly point of view, the Christian church in China was doomed. The mightiest forces that man could muster were arrayed against her. There was no lack of political power and military muscle to put down the Christian Church in that great land. But what was the result? After some fifty years of the most ruthless persecution by the most determined enemies armed with the most powerful weapons, the Christian Church in that country was not destroyed at all. It grew faster than the church in any other land. The official estimate of Christians in China today is upwards of 53,000,000. Without any physical power and might whatever, without even the ordinary means that the church usually enjoys, such as literature and worship facilities, the Christian Church in China was triumphant against its most powerful foes. How was this possible?

Undoubtedly this was possible only by the power and blessing of God, but he did not save it by some mighty miracle, like sending fire from heaven to destroy their enemies. On the contrary, it was saved by a power which we would be foolish not to recognise – the power of humble submission. There are ultimately no weapons, no guns or bombs that can be effective against this. It is a psychological, spiritual force that operates on a different level, so that it is unaffected by the blasts and smoke of physical force. It is this power that God himself used to destroy the power of Satan and to save the world from his tyranny. It is a paradox that takes the most powerful potentates by surprise, as the Lord said to St. Paul *"My strength is made perfect through weakness"* (II Corinthians 12:9).

If we study the cases where Jesus used the active positive power – the power to exert force and compulsion, we will see that he did so only when he was in a position of authority. For instance

15

when he healed the sick, cleansed the lepers, cast out demons and so on, he did so as one having authority. As the Son of God he certainly had authority over all illnesses, diseases, and demons. And so when it served the best interests of his people he healed them of their problems with his almighty power. The same goes for his turning water into wine, stilling of the storm, and raising the dead. As the Son of God he was in a position of authority over the elements, and over against death itself. He therefore performed such miracles as pleased him and no force was able to withstand him.

On the other hand, when he was under the authority of God whose will he was sent to perform, then he refused to use this almighty power, and submitted absolutely to the will of God. In the case of his crucifixion, Jesus knew that he had been sent into the world to suffer the punishment for man's sins. He had prayed to his Father in his anguish there in the garden of Gethsemane, *"Father, if it be possible let this cup pass from me: nevertheless not as I will but as thou wilt."* (Matthew 26:39). But when it was clear that it was his Father's will that he should suffer thus for the sins of the world, he absolutely refused to use his almighty power to help himself in any way, even when challenged to do so by the chief priests and elders.[14] Instead he seemed to act in utter weakness. His response to his heavenly Father was absolute submission. And yet in this way he won the victory over all his foes. The greatest victory that the world has ever seen.

And so it would seem that this must be our guide and rule too. Wherever we are in a position of power and authority over others or the things about us, we are free to use that active power that asserts itself with physical force, or compulsion and authority. Thus, for instance, God has given all people authority over the animals and the rest of creation,[15] parents have authority over their children, teachers over their students, governments over their citizens in civil matters and so on.[16] In these relationships it is appropriate for those in authority to use their power with a sense of responsibility. They can make demands and use threats as the occasion requires. They will, of course, do so with a sense of wisdom and justice, for the welfare of those placed under them. But in all other circumstances, when a person is in a position of inferiority or subjection to others – to government, parents, teacher and so on, he may not use this active power, any more than did our Lord. He must be ready to submit himself to those in authority, and ac-

---

[14] cp. Matt. 27:42f.

[15] cp. Gen. 1:26.

[16] cp. Rom. 13:1f.

cept what comes, even if he has to suffer through it.

That does not mean that he has no dignity, or that he is the mere play thing of those in authority, so that he must simply go down in utter defeat before them. On the contrary, he has the dignity that Christ himself showed in his suffering, and he still has that mighty power that Christ himself used – the strength that is made perfect in weakness. By humble submission to the powers that be, even to the point of suffering and death, he can exert great influence indeed. This is the power of humble Christian faith – the power that can move mountains, as Jesus said[17] the power that gave victory to the persecuted Christians in communist countries. This is the power by which Christ conquered all his foes, and won salvation for the world of sinners. This is the precious power that Christ has given to his Bride the Church in all her dealings with him. In her humble submission she will not only be victorious over all her foes, but will ultimately share in the glory and honour of Christ to live and reign with him for ever in heaven.

This is the mighty power that God has given to woman in relation to man, as we shall see soon. It is a power that can be successful for her where nothing else could succeed. It is her true potential and final answer to the positive power of man – a power against which man has no weapons and very little defence. It should be obvious that if woman seeks to answer man's positive power and authority by a similar show of power and authority, matching strength with strength, there would have to be a confrontation and a complete show-down in which she would be the ultimate loser. Even if she wins that battle by some super effort and determination or by the weakness of her rival, she will still have lost the war. Everything she gained by such strength and self-assertion will be lost in respect and dignity. She will finally succeed in destroying only herself for she will have lost her most valuable treasure – her glorious femininity and womanhood. On the other hand, if she responds to the positive power of man with the amazing, negative power of submission, by her very weakness, by her charming meekness and delicate submission she will exercise a mighty power that can conquer the strongest man, and by which he ultimately even delights to be conquered.

Marabel Morgan, in her excellent book, *The Total Woman,* has shown with numerous practical examples how it lies within the reach of every woman to make her husband absolutely adore her.[18]

[17] cp. Matt. 17:20

[18] The Total Woman, by Marabel Morgan. Hodder and Stoughton, 1975
   cp. p.27 et alia

If only women would study this power, and learn how to use it effectively, they would never want to, much less need to, resort to any other power in relation to man. Nothing else could be nearly as effective. This power that is made perfect in weakness is the paradoxical power of true femininity. It is a woman's peculiar forte. Though it may seem to her at first that it is a heavy yoke to have to submit to her husband, she will find, as Jesus promised, that her yoke is easy and her burden light,[19] for it is in the exercise of this power that a woman is most adored by man. It is when she thus surrenders herself to her husband in true meekness and submission that she shines forth as radiantly beautiful to him, and he will bow to her as his glorious queen.

---

[19] cp. Matt. 11:29-30

Chapter 4

THE BIBLICAL ARCHETYPE OF MARRIAGE

The Scriptures do not always spell out every truth in so many words, but they have a way of teaching by pictures and examples which may become clear only if we are familiar with those examples, or bother to find out what they are saying. This is certainly the case in the matter of the proper relationship between man and woman. The Bible teaches not only that they are fundamentally different, and that they are to have a complementary relationship in marriage and society, but instead of spelling this out in great detail, applying it to all the individual circumstances of life, it tells us that this relationship is to be like that between Christ and his Bride the Church. St. Paul says in Ephesians 5:25, *"Husbands, love your wives, as Christ also loved the church and gave himself for her."* (RSV). And, after speaking of the way husbands and wives should conduct themselves, he adds, *"This is a great mystery: and I take it to mean Christ and the church."* (RSV). To find out God's plan for husbands and wives, then, we will have to inquire, what sort of a relationship there is between Christ, the heavenly Bridegroom, and his Bride the Church, and then apply this to marriage. This is the unfolding of the mystery to which St. Paul points.

We should not think that this passage in Ephesians 5 is the only passage in the Bible that implies this. Nor is this simply a New Testament insight, but it was expressed and taught in numerous passages also in the Old Testament, wherever God's people – -his Church – -are likened unto a woman betrothed to him[20] or married to him. This is also the picture of the Church in several passages in Revelation where the Church is seen as the Bride, or the wife of the Lamb.[21] Incidentally the Church here, like in so many passages of Scripture, is not the earthly organisation of the various denominations and church bodies, but it is the communion of saints, as we confess in the Apostles' Creed – -that is the whole number of those who are true children of God, no matter what denomination they might come from.

This view of the Church, as the Bride of Christ, was, no doubt, in the mind of God already from the very beginning. It was one

---

[20] cp. Hos. 2:19ff.; Ezek.16 etc.
[21] Rev. 21:2; 21:9; Rev. 19:7.

19

of the reasons why he did not create Adam and Eve together, but created Adam first, and later created Eve from Adam's side. Already then, at their very beginning, life between the first man and woman was to be a picture of that between Christ and his Church. Christ, of course, existed first, and his Bride the Church came into being later. To accomplish this Christ had to die, going into a deep sleep, as did Adam, and shed his blood for her, his side being pierced, so that from this great sacrifice his Church might come into being. Because it was to cost Christ a tremendous price that his precious Bride, the Church, might be brought into existence, so it cost Adam something – his own rib, his own flesh and blood from his pierced side, so that Eve his wife could be created. Clearly this was no accident or unplanned circumstance, but it was surely part of God's plan right from the beginning. The creation of man and woman, with their human sexuality and relationship, was to be a little earthly picture, as it were, of the sublime heavenly relationship between Christ and his Church. Our sexuality – our masculinity and femininity – is only a dim, earthly reflection and image of the sublime, awe-inspiring, and majestic sexuality between Christ and his Bride the Church.

Those who think that our sexuality means nothing before God, and should have no significance in worship, or that God is neither male nor female, but some neuter form, have a totally unscriptural view not only of human sexuality, but also of the nature of God, and proceed to emasculate him in the interests of their own perverted understanding of sex. Throughout Scripture God has consistently revealed himself in masculine terms, so that, being the perfect, infinite God, we must know that he is what it really means to be masculine *par excellence*, and that our masculinity is only a faint earthly picture of that. Our sexuality is not unrelated to anything, but it is an image or earthly representation of his sexuality. That is why pornography is such a shocking evil. Those who think that pornography is simply exaggerating, and perhaps making fun of human sexuality, will never be able to understand why that should be so bad. If sex were simply a human or animal phenomenon, unrelated to anything beyond us, what would be so wrong with a bit of such "humour"? Would it be evil, for instance, to exaggerate or distort the tail of some animal in pictures? The matter is quite different when we realise that pornography not only distorts and brings disrepute upon human sexuality, but it is a desecration of God himself – a mockery of what is ultimately the archetype of our being, something far beyond our human understanding. Just as those who desecrate the flag of a country, insult and mock that country itself, (that is the whole purpose of it), so those who bring discredit upon human sexuality, ultimately desecrate God himself. They are meddling like children with realities far beyond their understanding.

It is to be hoped that no one reading this, is so devoid of deeper, spiritual understanding, or so incapable of spiritual analogy, that he would accuse the author of holding some gross, materialistic view of God, with huge physical sexual features and sexual lusts. God is a spirit and does not have physical attributes. We are dealing here with divine realities and principles that are spiritual archetypes of our physical sexuality. These realities are, as it were, the original prototypes or spiritual patterns from which our sexuality is derived. As the heart can be a physical representation or image of the immaterial emotions of love and affection, so our sexuality, though physical, may well be a representation of God's ultimate, spiritual masculinity. It is a shallow lack of perception or insight to see sexuality as centred upon, or even limited to physical features or representations of sex. These are rather only a physical expression of a much deeper reality.

A lead acid battery, with its negative and positive poles, is only one expression or instance of the far greater, universal principle of positive and negative polarity throughout nature. Because there are no leaden, positive and negative terminals in the sky, does not say that there is no polarity there. The lightning that lights up the whole sky, with the most awesome power and brilliant illumination, bears abundant testimony that there is indeed a negative and positive polarity of vast proportions out there of which our little battery is only one, tiny expression. So sexuality too – masculinity and femininity – is rather a deep, underlying principle of behaviour that has its expression in numerous ways, and our little physical, human sexuality, is only one, tiny aspect of that far greater sexuality, which the Scriptures ascribe to God himself, and more specifically to Christ, the heavenly Bridegroom, and his Bride the Church. If we want to understand and appreciate our own sexuality, and the proper relationship between the sexes here in this world, then we must surely see it in the context of its sublime archetype, the sexuality of Christ and His Church.

St. Paul in Ephesians 5 quotes from Genesis 2:24 *"For this reason a man shall leave his father and mother and be joined to his wife, and the two shall become one. This is a great mystery, and I take it to mean Christ and the church; however, let each one of you love his wife as himself, and let the wife see that she respects her husband."* (RSV). This assertion that the two shall become one, obviously refers to the institution of marriage, but then Paul makes the astounding statement, *"This is a great mystery, and I take it to mean Christ and the church."* In other words, the relationship between man and woman in marriage is a great mystery,

21

because it is a picture or representation of much deeper spiritual truths and principles – the Christ/Church relationship.

If this is true, then what help could distressed couples get from marriage guidance counsellors who don't even know anything about the relationship between Christ and his Church, and who would deny that it has anything whatever to do with marriage? At best such counsellors can be guided only by human observations, experience and psychology, which are not altogether irrelevant, but which fall far short of the real substance of sexuality itself. The very fact that marriage guidance counsellors are among those who have the highest incidents of marriage break-up and divorce, should tell us that, generally speaking at least, they have failed to see or understand the real substance of what true masculinity and femininity is all about. This is the mystery to which St. Paul points us in Ephesians 5, and this will therefore be the cue from which we shall attempt to learn something of what our sexuality ought to be, and how it should be expressed in the relationship between man and woman, particularly in marriage, but also in society.

St. Paul says in Ephesians 5:22-33: *"Wives, be subject to your husbands, as to the Lord. For the husband is the head of the wife as Christ is the head of the church, his body, and is himself its Savior. As the church is subject to Christ, so let wives also be subject in everything to their husbands. Husbands, love your wives, as Christ loved the church and gave himself up for her, that he might sanctify her, having cleansed her by the washing of water with the word, that the church might be presented before him in splendor, without spot or wrinkle or any such thing, that she might be holy and without blemish. Even so husbands should love their wives as their own bodies. He who loves his wife loves himself. For no man ever hates his own flesh, but nourishes and cherishes it, as Christ does the church, because we are members of his body. 'For this reason a man shall leave his father and mother and be joined to his wife, and the two shall become one.' This is a great mystery, and I take it to mean Christ and the church; however, let each one of you love his wife as himself, and let the wife see that she respects her husband."* (RSV)

Unfortunately this passage seems to infuriate many, because of the assertion of the apostle that wives are to be subject to their husbands as to the Lord, for the husband is the head of the wife. They read over the rest of the passage without noticing what it means for the husband to be the head of the wife, as St. Paul describes it, or what it really does for women. They fail to see that the ultimate purpose of such headship is that *"the church might be presented before him in splendour, without spot or wrinkle or*

any such thing, that she might be holy and without blemish."
(RSV). The Authorised version translates this, *"That he might present it to himself a glorious church, not having spot, or wrinkle, or any such thing; but that it should be holy and without blemish."*
While the husband is to be the head of the wife, with all the implications of this, yet the purpose of this is so that the wife may be the glory of her husband. In their relationship with each other he is to be the **head** and she is to be the **glory**.

This is stressed again in I Corinthians 11:7 where woman is said to be the glory of man. Surely no one can accuse the apostle Paul, much less the Holy Spirit (the real author of these teachings), of belittling or dishonouring women. If woman is to be the glory of man, that is about the highest honour that anyone can have. When people understand something of the responsibilities and sufferings implied by true headship, as in the case of Christ over his Church, on the one hand, and the sublime honour, distinction, and radiance prepared for woman, as the glory of man, on the other hand, virtually every woman will be glad to leave the matter of headship to her husband, and rejoice in the glory that is her special privilege. Overcome with a deep sense of awe and amazement, with profound honour and dignity, she will accept what the Lord has designed for her, put her hand to her mouth, bow her head meekly, and say with Mary, *"Behold the handmaid of the Lord; be it unto me according to thy word."* (Luke 1:38). This is the mystery that we need to be concerned about.

The argument of St. Paul in Ephesians 5 simply goes like this. If husbands want to know how to treat their wives, they should look to Christ and consider how he treats his Bride the Church, and then act that out in their relationship with their wives. If wives want to know how they should act towards their husbands, they should look to the Church, the glorious Bride of Christ, and consider how she acts towards Christ her Lord, and follow her example in their relationship with their husbands.

It is important to note also how St. Paul proceeds in this passage. First of all there is an admonition to women to subject themselves to their husbands, and then there is an admonition for husbands to love their wives as Christ loved the Church. It is the first admonition – the one to the wives – that contains the statement that the husband is the head of the wife. She is admonished to be subject to her husband because he is the head of the wife, as Christ is the head of the Church. In other words the reason for her submission to her husband, is because he is to be the head of his wife, as Christ is the head of the Church, and she, in her attitude and behaviour, is to want him to be the head. That is to say the headship of the husband is to be the concern of his wife. She

23

is to conduct herself in a way that this headship is possible and respected. This means that the love of a wife for her husband, and the way she treats him is to be concerned not for her own, selfish gain but for his honour and headship.

In the second admonition – the one to the husbands – the husband is required to love his wife with the kind of love that Christ showed to his Church, not so that he might be the head of his wife (that headship is not mentioned in this connection), or for any personal gain for himself, but so that his wife might attain her full glory. As the Church is presented to Christ *"a glorious church, not having spot or wrinkle, or any such thing,"* so his love is to seek to perfect his wife in all her splendour. As in the case of Christ, the husband's love for his wife is to be for her sake, and concerned for her welfare, not for his own. This is the nature of Christ's love, and it is to be the nature of a man's love for his wife.

Chapter 5

THE HUSBAND
AS THE HEAD OF THE WIFE

In studying the headship of the husband over his wife, it is important continually to bear in mind the fact that this headship is to be for her sake and not for his. Just as Christ's headship over his Church was not in any way for his own sake but for the sake of the Church,[22] so the leadership capacity of the husband, in all respects, is to redound to the benefit and blessing of his wife. That is its essential purpose.

What does St. Paul mean by calling the husband the head of the wife, as Christ is the head of the Church? The term "head" (kephale in Greek) is usually used to signify some sort of authority over others, but some have suggested that it could signify "source" or "origin". It would seem that nothing much is to be gained here by going into a deep investigation of this question. Ample investigation of that matter has been done by others,[23] and it seems that there is a far stronger case for the meaning of "authority" than for "source". If St. Paul had simply told us here that the husband is to be the head of the wife, we would need to be concerned with this matter to see what is actually meant by it. But that is not the case at all. St. Paul says rather that the husband is the head of the wife even as Christ is the head of the Church. And so whatever the word "head" means, we have to be concerned more about how Christ functions as the head of the Church. That, rather than the meaning of the word itself, will tell us how the husband is to be the head of his wife. And so we will be better occupied with considering the actual life and work of Christ for his Church. How does Christ function as head, and how does he express his headship over the Church?

If the headship of Christ implies authority over the Church, does he assert his pre-eminence and require everyone to cringe before him, saluting him in fear and trembling, as many earthly potentates may demand? Never! The very opposite is the case. And so no one can look to this passage of Scripture for support in his headship over his wife, if that is what he has in mind. Christ's headship is something quite different. It is rather an awesome responsibility which husbands can accept only in deep humility,

[22] cp. Eph. 5:27

[23] cp. Recovering Biblical Manhood and Womanhood by Wayne Grudem. Crossway Books,1991, p.425ff.

and with great self-sacrifice. It is intended for the benefit and blessing of his Church, and is to result in her ultimate glory. So also the headship of the husband over his wife, is not for his own exultation, but is for the benefit and blessing of his wife so that she might attain to her ultimate splendour and glory.

In his admonition to husbands St. Paul does not even mention their headship, let alone imply that they should be concerned about it and insist on due respect and honour on account of it. His headship is expressed and shows itself rather in demonstrating that sort of love for his wife that makes itself fully responsible for all her needs and wants, and which is determined to have her presented before him in her fullest glory, as Christ does for his Church.

THE NATURE OF CHRIST'S LOVE FOR THE CHURCH

Everything that Christ did for his Church was done in love for her. His whole approach to his Church, and the qualities that he showed in his dealing with her, were simply an expression of his great love for her. Above all, his sacrifice and death on the cross, was an expression of love for her, as Paul says, *"Christ loved the church and gave himself up for her."* (Ephesians 5:25). Similarly everything that a husband does for his wife – his whole attitude and approach to her, the exercise of his headship and authority, is to be an expression of his deep, self-sacrificing love for her.

Since the love of Christ for his Church, as her head, expresses itself differently than the love of the Church for Christ her Lord, we must conclude that his love is different in nature from the Church's love. Their love is not identical in nature, nor is it transposable. This is quite clear from St. Paul's words in Ephesians 5:22-32.

This has implications for the relationship between man and woman that may come as a surprise to some. Since, on the one hand, the love of a husband for his wife is to follow the pattern of the love of Christ for his Church, and since, on the other hand, the love of a wife is to be modelled on the love of the Church for Christ, and not the other way around, it is inescapable that the love of a man for his wife and the love of a wife for her husband, are to be different. They are not identical and can not simply be interchanged. In fact that is the whole point of St. Paul in Ephesians 5.

To understand how a husband is to love his wife, we need to understand how Christ regards his Church and acts towards her. What sort of love did he have for her? Did he simply have an affection or endearment for her that would last as long as he found her appealing, but would disappear if she became rebellious or uninteresting to him? This may be the sort of love that many husbands have for their wives, but Christ loved the Church with an overwhelming, self-sacrificing love that persisted through rebellion and wickedness. His love for her continued even when his anger was kindled against her because of her unfaithfulness, and he pursued her with his grace and forgiveness, even though it cost him his life.

That is how St. Paul tells us that husbands should love their wives too – *"as Christ loved the church and gave himself up for her"*. This requires true dedication and determination. It is easy enough for a man to love a woman when she is pleasant and beautiful, when she is cooperative and easy to get along with, but the matter is quite different when she is disgruntled and rebellious. Even then the husband is to love his wife with such a love that he would give himself up for her. Did Christ sacrifice himself for his church because she was so lovely, so faithful and obedient to him? Not at all. St. Paul tells us, *"God commendeth his love toward us, in that, while we were yet sinners, Christ died for us."* (Romans 5:8). That is the sort of love that Christ has for his Church. Even though we were sinners, living in rebellion against him, he gave himself for us in self-sacrificing love. So husbands are to love their wives too, as Christ loved the Church. Let no one imagine there will not be times when even an otherwise good and faithful wife will leave much to be desired in her attitude and approach to her husband. She may at times be anything but pleasant and lovable, and yet her husband is to love her nevertheless, as Christ loved his Church in spite of her sins.

But we should not fail to note also that the nature of Christ's love is out-going and self-sacrificing. Someone has said that there are three kinds of love: one in which there is nothing in it for the one being loved, only for the lover, as when a man says, "I love roast duck." Obviously there is nothing in that relationship for the duck, only for the man who eats it. The second love is when there is something in it for both parties, as when a couple love each other. This has mutual benefit. The third is a love in which there is nothing in it for the lover but only for the beloved. This is the love that Christ has for his Church. He loved her even though there was nothing in it for him. It cost him everything so that she might be saved. His love gives itself completely for the beloved, and will pay any price, and make any sacrifice for her welfare. It does not count the cost but commits itself fully and unreservedly to her. It says, as it were, I know what you need, I know what is required for your welfare, and that is what I shall provide, though it cost me my all – my very life. Christ gave his all for his

27

Church. He left his eternal glory with his Father in heaven, came to live among us in poverty and humility, and finally endured persecution and suffered the most cruel and shameful death for her on the cross. Nothing of all this was necessary for his own welfare. He was driven every inch of the way and moved at every moment by self-sacrificing love. Not what was good for him, but what was necessary for her was his only concern. That is the sort of love that a husband is to have for his wife if he is to be her head, as St. Paul says here. He must be ready first to be able to see what is good for her – what is necessary for her welfare, and then be ready to provide that even though it cost him all, as it did Christ. Nor will he allow this to cause resentment against her, when it spoils his plans, and hurts his pocket, but he will do what is necessary with the utmost, loving concern and devotion.

This does not mean that he must make ridiculous sacrifices just to satisfy her whims and fancies, but it does mean that no sacrifice will be too great to take care of her real needs and welfare. He will be prepared to go without many things that he would like; he will be prepared to sacrifice his savings for her, if that is necessary, so that she is properly cared for. She is the one that matters most to him, and her welfare calls for his ungrudging love and generosity. It is a love which gives itself completely and unreservedly to its partner and takes the full responsibility for her no matter what the cost.

It is a part of truly mature and responsible masculinity not to demand the services of his wife in return for his self-sacrifice for her. He does not do his share so that she might do hers, but he simply gives of himself in generous self-sacrifice in such a way that he requires nothing in return.[24] In this way he will call forth a response from her that will be much more glorious than anything that he could demand. She will be moved to shine forth in her glory because she cannot be in his presence without reflecting something of his light, and this will be a thousand times more important to him than any "fair share" that she might be required to contribute to their relationship.

Love, if it is genuine, will never force a good response. It must ever allow for the possibility of being rejected and spurned. Since God is the very essence of love, he is ready to give and sacrifice all for us, whether or not there is any favourable response from man. Most people in fact utterly reject his love and his great sacrifice for them. But he is loving and gracious to them nevertheless, and continues to offer them all the blessings that he has won for mankind. Any response must come not from compulsion, or

---

[24] cp. Lk. 6:35

from a duty to do our share, but from a free choice to respond to his love with thanks and gratitude.

That is the sort of love that a man is to have for his wife too. It may seem utterly unfair to him that he should be required to give himself, and to love self-sacrificingly without demanding any response or reward for all this, but that is the nature of the love of Christ which he is to have for his wife as her head. He is to give himself up for her, as Paul says, whether she responds or not. To be sure, it is most painful, if there is no response. It is an arrogant insult, as it is to Christ when his love is spurned. But it is most precious and sweet, to experience a true response which was not demanded or required out of obedience, but which is freely given out of genuine appreciation and gratitude for his love. St. John says of Christ, *"We love him because he first loved us."* (I John 4:19). This is the sort of feminine love that a man needs from his wife too, a love that is not demanded but is spontaneous as the result of his giving himself for his wife. Unless man can show this sort of undemanding, self-sacrificing love for his wife, he can not claim to love her as her head, as Christ loved his Church.

Girls sometimes complain that they find themselves being pursued and loved by a young man whom they simply don't like. They may do their best to put him off, even resorting to rudeness and nasty behaviour. This can go on for months and even for years, and yet he still continues to make advances to them. They begin to detest and even to hate him. The more he loves such a girl the more she actually hates him. How should the love of a man react in such a situation? It is the very nature of true love that it will never try to compel a favourable response. It simply risks all, including utter rejection. And if that should be the response it must finally accept it graciously and say, as it were, "I love you too much to force you to do anything against your will. If you don't want me and my love, then so be it. I shall let you alone completely and forever." It is a woman's privilege to reject a man's love.

Incidentally, here we have the answer to the age-old question, how can a God of love allow anyone to be eternally lost in hell? God, of course, loves all sinners. Not only has he provided free salvation for them, but he pursues them with the Gospel and reveals his love to them in many ways. But it is the privilege of sinners to reject his love and salvation. Many do not want to be loved by God. The more he loves them and shows his love by pursuing them, the more they hate him. They simply want God to leave them alone. God's love will never force anyone to love him against their will, and though it deeply hurts him to be rejected by those whom he loves he will finally say to them, as it were, "If that is the way you want it, that is the way it shall be. Thy will be done. Depart from me ye cursed."[25] True love simply has to let them go. Nobody will ever be able to accuse God of a lack of love for allowing the wicked to go with Satan to hell. He loved them too much to force them to come with him to heaven against their will.

Like Christ, a husband knows too that his joy and happiness can be realised only in his wife's welfare and blessing. It is doubtful whether a loving husband can ever be happier than his wife. Only when she is happy and contented, can he be truly happy. He may laugh and joke with his friends; he may go on outings with them, but as long as he knows that his wife is miserable and in trouble he will not be truly happy. His golfing or fishing with his friends will not relieve his pain at the suffering and trouble of his wife. The only way for him to find relief is to sacrifice himself for her, and do for her what is necessary that she may be truly happy and cheerful. He takes the risk of getting nothing in return. But he does not want to buy any of her graces or demand her love; it must come freely or not at all.

This does not give the wife the right to use her smiles and graces as a weapon to hold her husband under siege, as it were. She dare not try getting her husband to do whatever she wants. She may not make his life miserable with petty demands and desires. He can see through such pettiness and will not respect her for it. True benevolence is not a response to pushy demands, much less to threats, but it comes from seeing what is necessary, what is cherished, and being ready to provide that freely, without requiring any response at all.

It is a distortion of Christianity, in fact a sign of spiritual sickness, to think that the Christian may put pressure on Christ by means of all sorts of pressure methods in prayer, for instance. It was the prophets of Baal who cried out in desperation, and cut themselves with knives till the blood gushed out upon the altar, so as to win the pity of their god and get him to do what they required, namely to send fire from heaven to burn up their sacrifice.[26] If Christians resort to pressure methods in prayer, to get the Lord to do as they require of him, or if they try to put him under moral obligation to hear them, and grant their requests, they are violating the proper Christ/Church relationship. The Lord will not thus allow himself to be manipulated, and those who try to do so need not think that Christ will do as they want. The true Christian simply leaves everything in God's hands and knows that he will do what is best for him, even if he must suffer. And therefore he will turn to God in thanks and praise for whatever

[25] cp. Matt. 25:41

[26] cp. I Kings 18:26-28

God gives. It is the very nature of true, masculine love to be benevolent, to be self-sacrificing for the sake of the beloved, and to want to make her happy, but it will not be blackmailed by false claims or threats.

CHRIST THE SAVIOUR OF THE CHURCH

The first expression of Christ's love for his Church mentioned by St. Paul is that he is the Saviour of the Church. This must imply that he sees her as being in need of help and salvation, and elects to provide that help for her. All of mankind, of whom the Church is made up, were sinners, doomed to eternal punishment in hell, and would certainly have had to suffer that punishment eternally, had it not been for the great love of Christ our Saviour. He therefore took it upon himself to do everything necessary to save us. He became our substitute and did for us what we should have done, fulfilling the law of God for us and suffering the punishment for our sins so that we could be saved.

How then should the husband perform this function of Christ's love in being a saviour to his wife? There is no need for him to save her from sin. Christ has already done that. But he will see her as being in need of help in many respects simply because of her nature. Her femininity makes her more vulnerable than he, so that she needs his protection. She has many needs that he does not. He could live in a rough environment with few conveniences that would make it most difficult for her, because of her nature. He therefore sees himself as the one who must take the responsibility for these things and provide the necessary help for her. If she brings trouble upon herself, possibly because of her own folly and weakness, he does not leave her to her own devices, and insist that, since she got herself into this mess, it is up to her to get herself out of it as best she can. No, like Christ he becomes her saviour by taking the full responsibility of her faults upon himself, putting himself in her position, and as her substitute, does what she should have done, and suffers for her what she should have suffered.

Here already we see a great weakness in man, who fails to act like Christ to his wife. So many men, in our experience, when their wife is given to some folly or has acted foolishly in some way, utterly refuse to act as her saviour. They do one of two things. Either they try to justify the wrongs of their wife, so that she does not lose face (Christ did not justify the sins of mankind), or they insist that their wife get herself out of her own mess. They don't want to be seen as having any responsibility for it. They will talk to their mates in the pub about their wife, making remarks about how stupid women can be. They will remember the faults of their

31

wife, and occasionally make joking remarks about it even before others, as a sort of dig to impress her and others of their own superiority. This is not the way of Christ our Saviour in his love for us. He took our sin and guilt upon himself and bore the punishment for all of us as our Saviour. Now that we have been saved and justified he defends us against the accusations of Satan. So the husband needs to learn from Christ not only to take the full responsibility for all his wife's faults, in the sense that he acknowledges them and bears the blame and the cost for them, but also in the sense that he, having relieved her of the guilt and blame, actually sees her and treats her as justified before him, so that he takes her part, answers the criticism from others against her, and defends her with all his being. To touch her, or in any way to slight and criticise her, is to criticise him, so that anyone who wants to insult her must deal with him. He stands between her and the entire world. There is no way to deal with her apart from through him. Of course this is not easy, and it may not be pleasant. It would be much easier for a man to let his wife fend for herself, and bear the insult and reproach of the world, especially if that is deserved.

But this saving love goes even deeper. To be the Saviour of his Church, Christ had to accept responsibility not only for all her sins before the world, but also before God. So the husband, as head of his wife, is to accept responsibility before God for her, and be held accountable to God for her. Note that after Eve had led Adam into sin, and God came to confront them, he did not call to Eve to give an account of her sin. He called to Adam. We read that *"The Lord God called unto Adam, and said unto him, Where art thou?"* (Genesis 3:9). And then he continued to interrogate Adam regarding this matter. Nor does Adam complain to the Lord and say, as it were, "Look this is not fair. It was Eve that got us into this mess. You ought to be dealing with her." No he could not get away with such a dodge in the presence of God. God knew, and so did he, that he was accountable for the whole sad business before God, and that he had to answer for it. He could not save Eve from her sin, because that was impossible for man, but neither could he disclaim responsibility for it. God held him to account, and he had to face it as the responsible head of woman. So God will hold every husband to account for his wife and family. Even though she or they may be the initiators of error or evil, yet it is the husband as head, who will have to give an account to God. That is simply one of the responsibilities of headship. The husband is accountable to see to it that his wife and family are true and faithful to their Lord. If he has tried diligently to lead them to be faithful to Christ, but they refused, they will suffer for it, because he can not atone for their sin, but he will have saved his soul. Nevertheless he is responsible before God. This is much like the case of the watchmen and the prophets who were responsible to warn the people of an approaching enemy or of God's wrath. If they failed to sound a proper warning, they would be held responsible and be punished. God required the people's blood at their hand. But if they warned the people and they did not heed, the people would perish, but they would have saved their own soul.[27] Headship carries with it the same awesome responsibilities. Only a truly self-sacrificing love can accept them.

CHRIST THE INITIATOR

St. Paul's direction that *"the husband should love his wife even as Christ loved the church, and gave himself for her,"* carries a freight of precious truths for our instruction. The fact that Christ in his love for the Church **gave** himself for her, expresses the truth that it is the nature of the love of Christ as the head of the Church to take the initiative. To give is simply to be the initiator, the one who acts, and whose action calls for a response. This too is to be the nature of the love of a husband for his wife. The love of a man is an outgoing, active giving of himself, to woo or to win his beloved. It wants to make her his own and to take the full responsibility for her. The love of a woman for man, or for her husband, on the other hand, is rather the desire to belong to him, to be the object of his love and attention.

While some may deny this, it is a truth that should be obvious to everyone because of the very physical nature of man and woman. Surely we can learn truths not only from educated teachers and from experience, but often by simply having a good look at what we are talking about. Anyone who has looked in the bathroom mirror and dared to ask the obvious question why he or she is the way he or she is, can not but be struck with the truth that man is intended to be the giver – the initiator, and woman the receiver – the responder. Our physiology is not what it is by pure accident, bearing no relationship to the overall nature of man and woman, but it is rather intended to be a picture of deep and precious truths about ourselves, to teach us truths that affect our whole life and being – what it really means to be man and woman.

This also belongs to the very essence of what it means for the husband to be the head of the wife. He is the initiator in their relationship, the one who takes the lead, not for his sake, as we have

---

[27] cp. Ezek. 33:1-9

seen, but for the sake of the one whom he loves. This is so in almost every respect. The husband as the head of the wife takes the lead in their home, in providing for their needs, in sustaining their life together, in protecting them and their family, in their business and financial pursuits, and in their religious life. He does this not because he considers himself to be greater or more important, but for the sake of the one he loves. The very nature of his love for her can not wait around for something to happen, but initiates what he knows to be for her good. It accepts the full responsibility for his beloved and is determined to carry it out. It is the very nature of feminine love, on the other hand, to want it so. She wants to be the object of his aggressive love. She wants to be protected, provided for, sustained and led by someone whose love is responsible for her. She is glad to have her husband take the initiative and to entrust herself to his leadership because of his love for her.

This does not mean to say that a truly loving husband will simply lead in his own way, without taking into account the desires and suggestions of his wife. True leadership, as in the case of Christ, is never concerned with demonstrating superiority, but with being responsible for what is best for the beloved. Christ humbled himself, even before the misguided leaders of the church, and suffered insult at their hands, in order to do what was necessary for the welfare of his Church. So the husband too, will not hesitate to humble himself before his wife and listen to her suggestions. He is not concerned about maintaining face or an appearance of superiority before her. In fact it is rather a confession of weakness always to insist on his own way, and demand that his ideas must prevail. It is usually the little boys at school who are short by comparison with their own age group, who are always ready to punch and impress themselves on others. Because they are weak or at some disadvantage they think they have to impress others. Stronger lads don't need to make such an impression. They can afford to be gracious. So the husband, who is truly a man, and a genuine leader of his wife, does not need to act tough to make an impression, or to demand respect. Because he is a truly responsible leader, he can afford to take into account the wishes and desires of his wife and family. Even if he believes his own ideas, in a certain project, may have been better, yet, if the welfare of his wife and family is not at stake, he may, in his very capacity as leader, concede to his wife's wishes or the wishes of his children. This does not detract from his headship or from his initiative, but is simply a demonstration of his magnanimous leadership capacity, to lead even in paths not chosen or preferred by him.

34

Any claim of headship which seeks to put down or eliminate personal initiative in others so that his authority is not challenged, and which even resorts to oppressive, overbearing supervision of his wife, finally reveals a deep incapability or weakness, and a lack of true love and responsibility. While Christ in his Word, has given his Church a clear, authoritative lead and direction − which he expects her to follow absolutely, and which she will willingly do, yet Christ has not regulated everything or given his Church laws for every activity and belief. While the Church accepts the Word and authority of Christ in all things, yet most of the things in life are matters of indifference where Christ has neither commanded nor forbidden a particular action. There the church may follow her own initiatives and exercise her good common sense. In doing so she also shows herself to be truly faithful and committed to her Lord. This in no way undermines the headship or authority of Christ over his Church. So also with the relationship between the husband and wife. Even though, as the initiator, the husband gives general leadership and direction, yet he delights to leave as much as possible to the preferences of his beloved wife, and is thrilled to see her exercise her special feminine choices. This allows her to be herself, and to express her femininity. This does not pose any threat to his ultimate headship at all. It rather leads his wife to exult in his leadership, and to accept it with confidence and trust. In this way she never feels threatened or oppressed, but rather protected and nourished.

In case of real disagreement between husband and wife, in matters where he believes the welfare of his wife or family is at stake, the husband will not abdicate his responsibility as head, but he will accept the onerous burden of the final say, and do what he believes to be in their best interest and welfare. This is simply responsible love. It should not be seen as a victory over his wife, or an opportunity to teach her who is boss, but as his unenviable, loving responsibility because he is the one who must finally give an account. This is a special occasion and opportunity to demonstrate his great love for her − to let her see that he would rather die than see her come to any hurt. The truly feminine wife too will want it that way, and will not turn away in bitter resentment, hoping that her husband is wrong and will make a fool of himself so that she is in a stronger position next time. She will accept his leadership and seek to make his decision work as best she can.

CHRIST PROVIDES FOR HIS CHURCH

One very important way in which Christ shows his love for the Church is to provide for her. Ultimately it is Christ who feeds and nourishes his Church with the bread and water of life − the Word and sacraments, so that she might live through him. Jesus assured the woman at the well that he provides the water of life that will be *"a well of water springing up into everlasting life."* (John 4:14). Two chapters later Jesus said to his disciples, *"Except ye eat the flesh of the Son of man, and drink his blood, ye have no life in you. Whosoever eateth my flesh, and drinketh my blood, hath eternal life; and I will raise him up at the last day. For my flesh is meat indeed, and my blood is drink indeed."* (John 6:53-55). Without going into the full meaning of this amazing passage it is clear that Jesus claims to be the one who provides the true meat and drink for his Church. He is the provider of his Church, to the extent that those who accept his nourishment will live eternally, but those who refuse to accept his providence will die.

This is also to be part of the responsibility of the husband in his love for his wife. He is to provide for her. This was already implied in the Creation and Fall accounts. Not only did woman have her life from man – being his own flesh and blood, so that she was really taken from him and had her life from his,[28] but Adam was to provide for the continued welfare of his wife, working the ground and growing food for their sustenance.[29] This was not the result of the curse, in consequence of sin, it was there already before sin entered into the world, as the wording of the curse makes clear,[30] but the curse made this task onerous and difficult, whereas it would have been most pleasurable before that, in the state of bliss.

All this does not mean that the wife may not do anything towards her own providence or even that of the family. She may delight in growing fruit and vegetables for the family, or there may be times and economic conditions when this becomes necessary. Her husband may even be incapacitated so that she has to assume this role completely, at least for a time. But this will be done on the understanding that it is part of his role as head of the family, and that it is only their misfortune or need that makes this necessary. The husband will feel disappointed that he is unable to do his duty towards his wife fully, and will give her all the moral support and encouragement he can as she does what is really his responsibility in this situation.

The matter is quite different when a wife simply asserts that it is her right and privilege to provide for herself. This amounts to a declaration of independence, which is the opposite of marriage, in fact a negation of it, and a rejection of the headship of

---

[28] cp. Gen. 2:23

[29] cp. Gen. 3:17-19

[30] cp. Gen. 3:17-19

man. The matter is even more aggravated when the wife wants to earn her own money and have her own bank account so that she can do what she likes with her own money to buy the things that she wants for herself. This may sound perfectly innocent in a society that likes to stress the independence of the individual, but it is anathema to the biblical concept of marriage. It is a clear declaration of a degree of independence that is the very opposite of marriage. The Lord intended marriage to be a *"one flesh"* relationship. *"They are no longer two, but one,"* (Matthew 19:6. RSV) as Jesus says. If they are in fact one and not two, then it is impossible, by definition, for one partner to have something that does not belong to the other, or to have some area of independence that is not the business and responsibility of the other. Unless we are ready to dispose of the biblical concept of marriage, it must be granted that everything that the husband has, also belongs to his wife, and conversely everything that the wife has is also the property of her husband. St. Paul makes it quite clear that even their very persons – their own bodies; do not belong to themselves but to their partners. He says, *"The wife does not rule over her own body, but the husband does; likewise the husband does not rule over his own body, but the wife does."* (I Corinthians 7:4). If this is true of their very bodies, how much more so of everything else? There is and can be no such thing as independence between partners in marriage. This does not mean to say that a marriage is necessarily doomed the moment any such independence is allowed. But it does say that it is a departure from the biblical concept of marriage, and that a marriage which tolerates such independence will be all the poorer and less glorious as a result. It will cease, in this respect, to be a reflection of the relationship between Christ and his Bride, where he and she are one – he the head, and she the body. It is, to this extent, a desecration of the great archetype of which it was intended to be a type.

Incidentally, apart from the violation of the divine archetype, which is ultimately an insult to God, it should be obvious that the push to have married women in the work force on an equal basis with men is the greatest single factor causing unemployment in our modern society. This is simply a cold, mathematical fact. There probably never was a time in the history of our nation when there was full employment in the sense of having everyone in the work force. That both husband and wife should be allowed to earn an income, when thousands of others are unemployed, and have to be maintained by the state with taxpayer's money, is not only economic folly, but far worse than that, it may well spell the social destruction of the nation. For young men to be unemployed is fearfully demoralising, and the longer this is allowed to continue the higher the price to be paid for this ideological experiment.

CHRIST ADORNS HIS CHURCH

The providence of the husband for his wife is to extend far further than merely supplying her essential needs in the sense of food to eat and clothing to keep her warm. According to the love which Christ shows for his Church, which the husband is to emulate, he is also to adorn and perfect her as Christ does his Church. This is quite clear from St. Paul's words: *"Husbands, love your wives, as Christ loved the church and gave himself up for her, that he might sanctify her, having cleansed her by the washing of water with the word, that the church might be presented before him in splendour, without spot or wrinkle or any such thing, that she might be holy and without blemish. Even so husbands should love their wives as their own bodies."* (Ephesians 5:25-28. RSV). Not only has Christ done everything to provide what is essential for the salvation of his Church, but he also sanctifies or perfects her for himself. He washes away all her sins in holy baptism. He clothes her with his own perfect righteousness – a righteousness[31] which exceeds the righteousness of the Scribes and Pharisees.

It is Christ through his Word and grace that adorns and perfects his Bride so that she might be presented before him in splendour. Notice that this is in the passive voice. She does not present herself before him in splendour, but she is presented before him in splendour. This adorning and perfecting of herself for him, is ultimately the work and concern of Christ her Lord.

So it is to be also in the relationship between a husband and his wife. It is to be his aim and purpose that she might appear before him in her best possible form *"without spot or wrinkle or any such thing. . . holy and without blemish."* A callous and indifferent husband, who is not concerned how his wife dresses and adorns herself, does not show the kind of love for his wife that Christ shows to his Church. If he is not interested in such things, and simply leaves it all to her, such a husband has abdicated from his loving responsibility as head.

In the light of this it is a very unfortunate custom among some brides to prepare their wedding dress without consulting their bridegroom, or even refusing to let him see it till the day of their wedding. It is not the Church, but Christ the Bridegroom, who provides the wedding dress for his Bride. This is not the self-chosen works or self-righteousness of Christians, but rather the perfect garments of Christ's righteousness. Christ adorns his Bride with his own righteousness. It would be much more fitting, therefore, for Christian brides to have their husbands provide their wedding dress.

---

[31] cp. Matt. 5:20

The refusal of some brides to let their husbands see their dress before their wedding, thinking it will be a pleasant surprise for him, is not only contrary to the example of Christ and his Church, but an ill-informed risk. They may well discover that their husband is not at all impressed with their self-chosen wedding dress, so that their whole day is spoiled. The hurt that they both suffered through it will forever be remembered, and impressed upon them by their wedding photos. The same principle applies to the hairdo and other adornments of the bride. Most husbands quickly develop a taste as to how their loved one looks best and are only jarred by something too different. What was intended to be a pleasant surprise, may well become a shock that will hurt the wife most of all as she feels that she is not appreciated in what was to be the crowning glory of her life.

It may well be true, that, at least initially, a young husband doesn't know anything about women's dresses and adornments. He may never have taken much notice of such things. His girlfriend looks beautiful to him, and that is all that matters. Perhaps she has good taste, and can generally present herself before him in a way that is very pleasing to him, and so he is happy to leave all of that to her. But that is not the way Christ's love deals with his Church, and that is not the way the love of a mature man will treat his wife either. If he loves her deeply, he will be very concerned about what she wears and the way she adorns herself. Even though he might not have taken much notice of such things before he set his affections upon some special young lady, as soon as he begins to take the responsibility for her, his love for her will force him to take a vital interest in these things as well. Everything that concerns or touches his beloved in any way, touches him at the same time, and must be his concern too. This must be so just because they are one and will function as one.

Circumstances may alter cases, but generally the husband who simply lets his wife go off to buy a new dress for herself, as if that were none of his business, is either totally lacking in a sense of what is beautiful and pleasant, so that he can't tell the difference between beauty and ugliness, and therefore doesn't deserve a beautiful wife, or he is sadly lacking in the sort of love that Christ has for his Bride. It is a confession of utter poverty on his part. When she comes home with something that pleases her, and he does not even notice it, and hardly even looks at her, she has every reason to feel absolutely insulted and incensed at his insensitivity, and lack of appreciation for what she is and how she looks. That is probably even worse for her than if he sees her in her new dress and passes some remark that it is rather uninteresting. This might hurt her, but at least he did take some notice, and that is something. Next time he might consent to go with her and help her find something that really thrills him, so that she can appear before him in splendour. Eventually, as his love grows and matures, more like that of Christ, he will begin to take notice of these things himself, and find something that would do much for his wife. When he becomes efficient in this responsibility and loving care for his wife, he may begin of his own initiative, to bring home clothing for his wife that he believes would enhance her – things that would make her appear before him in splendour, as Christ provides for his Bride. This is the sort of love that he needs to learn from Christ the heavenly Bridegroom.

It is very possible that there may at times be instances where what a wife likes to wear, is really quite detestable to her husband. He believes it makes her look sloppy, or old and grannyish, when he wants her to appear radiantly fresh and beautiful. What then? Should he take the attitude that it is her body and so she can wear what she likes? Any husband who takes that attitude has renounced the love of Christ for his Church. That is not how Christ loves his Church. He does not allow her to adorn herself with her own self-chosen works or self-righteousness, but insists that she be clothed with the garments of his righteousness. So the husband too, if he truly loves his wife, will insist that she be clothed in a way that makes her appear truly beautiful to him. It is not simply her body that she is dealing with but his. He and she are one.

This is the case not only with clothing, but with everything touching the appearance of his wife – the way she does her hair, the kind of make-up she wears, her fingernails, eyebrows, jewellery, everything. She is his precious "rib" as Luther used to say. *"The wife does not rule over her own body, but the husband does."* as St. Paul puts it (I Corinthians 7:4 RSV). Ultimately, perhaps after a period of disappointment, in which she feels sorry for herself that she can not wear a particular dress or hairstyle, that hurts her husband, she will find that she gets much more joy and satisfaction in appearing before him in the clothes that he likes and adorned in a way that really delights him, than parading before him in something that he resents and makes him turn away from her.

That is just how it is also with our relationship to Christ too. There are Christians who believe they are doing excellent works pleasing to Christ, running about organising ladies auxiliary teas, and church functions, but neglecting their home and family. With their self-chosen, popular and more glamorous works, in the public eye, they might think that God ought to be very pleased with them, and they might feel deprived and disappointed when they

40

learn that God would rather have them do their simple duty that he has laid upon them, looking after their husband and family in the home, making that a precious haven of peace and rest for their family. But they will ultimately glorify their Lord better and receive his praise and blessing if they simply do what he has laid upon them. He who is greatest in the kingdom of heaven finally, may not be some up-front church official, or medical missionary, but may well be some lowly housewife who served her husband and family in meekness and faithfulness, making her home a little picture of the heavenly relationship that Christ has prepared for us.

Incidentally, even though this is not strictly the place to point it out, we might note in passing that St. Paul asserts not only that the wife does not rule over her own body, but the husband does; but he also goes on immediately to assert, *"likewise the husband does not rule over his own body, but the wife does."* (I Corinthians 7:4 RSV). This means that while the wife is to submit everything touching her person to the will and authority of her husband, he is to do the same, and commit himself and his person to the authority of his wife. This is one area in which it would seem, at least on the surface, that the relationship between Christ and his church is not a strict guide for everything in marriage. It is difficult to imagine the Church having authority over anything concerning the person of Christ. And yet this seems to be what the apostle is saying in the relationship between a husband and wife. *"The husband does not rule over his own body, but the wife does."* This must mean that the wife is able to insist upon her preferences with respect to her husband's body. If she does not like him to have tattoos or a beard, she has every right to insist that her wishes be respected. He does not rule over his own body but she does. This has quite extensive application.

It is true that what St. Paul is saying here is applied directly to sexual relations. In fact he says in the very next verse, *"Do not refuse one another except perhaps by agreement for a season, that you may devote yourselves to prayer; but then come together again, lest Satan tempt you through lack of self-control."* But this does not limit the wife's rule over her husband's body to the area of sex. Not at all. Paul argues from the greater to the less. Since each partner has authority over the body of their partner (which is far more than sex) they ought not to refuse sexual relations, which is only a small part of bodily functions. We have no right to restrict such statements more narrowly than they are presented in Scripture. It is a fundamental principle of biblical interpretation that we must allow a passage of Scripture the full scope of its legitimate inference, unless it is clearly limited by the context or some

41

other passage of God's Word. According to this principle it would seem that St. Paul's words must be taken to imply that the husband's body or person is to be within the authority of his wife, however embarrassing this might seem to be to the main thesis of this book, since the Church does not rule over the person of Christ her Lord. Who knows at this stage, since we are dealing here with a great mystery, as St. Paul says, there may even be ways in the heavenly marriage relationship, that it will please Christ to accommodate himself to the sanctified preferences of his glorious Bride. There are many things which we can not know now.

The great love of Christ for his Church, and his determination to sanctify her, and have her presented before him in splendour, without spot or wrinkle or any such thing,[32] surely shows that he cherishes his Church and is proud of her. He not only wants to adorn and beautify her for himself but when he speaks of his Church he does so in glorious and exulted terms. He portrays her as radiantly beautiful. In Revelation 12 she is portrayed as a glorious *"woman clothed with the sun, with the moon under her feet, and on her head a crown of twelve stars."* (Revelation 12:1). Later the Church is described not only as adorned in *"fine linen bright and pure"*,[33] but she is described in terms of the most precious stones and jewellery.[34] In his letters to the churches in Rev. 2 and 3, the Lord also praises the good qualities of his church wherever this is possible. He praises the Christians' works, their toil, their patient endurance, their rejection of error, their patience in tribulation, poverty, hatred and slander, their love, faith, service and so forth. And he encourages them to continue in these graces.

Perhaps it might seem strange to us that Christ could actually praise us for our good works and Christian graces. We who are wretched sinners, cleansed and sanctified only by his mercy, have become the objects of his pleasure, so that he even praises and encourages us.

If that is how Christ, in his great love, sees his Church and deals with her, the husband too must also see and treat his wife in a similar way. Not only is he, like Christ, to adorn her and perfect her, so that she is presented to him in glory and splendour, but his conduct towards her and the way he addresses her, is to be in keeping with the glory and splendour with which he adorns her. Every husband needs to learn to refer to his wife, especially in public but also in private, in exalted terms. Many husbands

---

[32] cp. Eph. 5:25-27

[33] cp. Rev. 19:8

[34] cp. Rev. 21: 2; 9; 15ff.

who call their wife "darling", possibly as a sort of hangover from more romantic days, will refer to her as "the missus", the "old woman", or even "the boss" when they are with their mates. This is most un-Christlike. They ought to refer to her only in exalted and respectable terms for their own sake, for her sake, and for the sake of their friends. For a wife to hear herself being referred to in such derogatory terms, is most humiliating, and not only undermines her confidence in her husband and his attitude to her, but also undermines her self-respect. It also teaches others to have a low view of their partners when they hear wives referred to in derogatory terms. Even if this is done "for fun" or with a chuckle, it is nevertheless un-Christlike and undignified, and ought to be beneath the mature, loving head who sets the standards for his family and must give an account. A wife who is consistently referred to by her husband in exulted terms will also think more highly of herself and try to be still more pleasing to him because she knows she is appreciated.

After all the vulgarism that is written on T-shirts, it was most refreshing to see one man proudly wearing a shirt bearing the name of his wife in big letters, "MARILYN'S MAN". In this way he was telling the world how he regarded his wife — that he was most proud of her. I can't recall ever having met her but I know that she was glad to be his wife simply because he made it obvious that she was most precious to him. Husbands will do well to show a bit of ingenuity in highlighting their wives and holding them up as precious and glorious to the world. The delightful response of feminine commitment and self-surrender will well reward their efforts.

Today courtesy and chivalry are deliberately being misunderstood and misinterpreted as if it were an attempt to make women look weak in comparison with men. If a man holds the coat of his wife as she puts it on, or opens the car door for a lady, they pretend that it makes it look as if the lady is too weak to do such things herself. Nonsense! This is a deliberate distortion of a rebellious mind. Such courtesy, as everyone knows, is simply a man's way of saying that he cares for his wife profoundly, and delights in taking the trouble to help her. It shows something of that self-sacrificing love that is so necessary in the relationship between man and woman. We need to practice such courtesy far more, not because it comes from the Victorian era, but because it is a small demonstration of a Christ-like attitude to women.

One of the most subtle enemies of marital happiness is a complacency and indifference that simply takes the beloved for granted after marriage. This was well expressed by that callous, insensitive mere male, when his wife, pining for lack of evidence that she was loved and appreciated, finally asked him, "Do you love me?" He answered in an irritated voice, "Look I told you years ago, on the day I married you, that I loved you, and I expect you to take me seriously, and believe what you are told. Now don't ask me again." The point is that true love, in as much as it is genuine, will not simply make statements about itself, but will never cease to express itself in innumerable ways. Where such loving expression is lacking, there a wife has reason to doubt whether her husband still loves her.

Some years ago, a man whose marriage was breaking up, came to the author and shared some of his problems. He told how his wife did not appreciate what he did for her. He had gone out of his way to provide for her so well. He had bought her a new colour TV. He had bought her an excellent sewing machine, given her money to get herself new dresses, and new curtains in the lounge and numerous things. He did these things for her often at great sacrifice to himself, and yet she complained and was not happy. Whatever could be wrong with the woman? What more did she expect? He was not a wealthy man and was doing all he could for her. In pity I looked at him and said, "When did you last touch her? When did you last put your arms around her and lavish your love upon her? When did you last show her that you adore her person, and appreciate her for what she is?" He looked puzzled. I am not sure that he would still have had the courage to take her into his arms, look down into her eyes and lips, and gently stroke her eyebrows, in sheer amazement and adoration for what God had given him. But I do know that it certainly would have done far more for her than a new colour TV. She could have had thousands of such demonstrations of his love for a fraction of the cost of a new TV, and it would have been much more appreciated. A wife needs to be reassured often that her husband delights in her, is proud of her, and that he adores her person for what she is. It is no good a man claiming to be self-sacrificing in his love for his partner because he is prepared to spend money on her, but will not show and demonstrate his love for her in such simple and most natural ways. Only when such love is obvious and demonstrated daily will the larger sacrifices be appreciated. It is the little things in life that show the true condition of our heart, and that are finally the most important in our relationship with our partner. The widow's mites were a much better demonstration of her love for her Lord than the large gifts of the rich, as Jesus pointed out.[35]

At the present time the Church can not see Christ her Bridegroom at all. She is attracted to him not because of what she can see of him, (The pictures that artists draw of Christ may not be at all accurate) but because of what he has done and still does for her – his work of redemption and salvation. Christ, on the other hand, can see his Church, and is intent on perfecting her for himself.

As the Church appreciates Christ for what he has done, so woman appreciates man more for what he does rather than for what he is or looks like. His personal appearance is usually nothing startling. Few people would spend time admiring a man's various features. It is what he does that makes him delightful, someone to be admired, to be respected and honoured. With a woman it is the other way around. Like the Church she is appreciated largely for what she is rather than for what she does. In fact what she does simply enhances and draws attention to what she is. Even most of the sports in which women engage, including tennis and basketball, but especially skating and dancing, serve to emphasise and impress upon us what woman is. She is the object of attention and everything that she does draws attention to herself. Even when she walks or sings or reads or plays a violin, this draws attention to her person, simply because of her femininity. She can hardly do anything without drawing attention to herself. This is wonderful. This is how it should be. She was made to be noticed and adored by man. This is part of her glory. But if she is going to find joy and satisfaction in life, she has to know and feel that she is appreciated for what she is. It is therefore the responsibility of every loving husband to give her this assurance by continual expressions of appreciation. He needs to make her glad to be a woman. When he fails in this she is bound to feel unwanted and useless. She may even hate herself and try to make her husband hate her too. The satisfaction and meaning that she had hoped to find in life and marriage will therefore not be realised and the marriage will be under threat.

It is interesting that the Bible teaches us that the good works that the Christian does may be ever so simple and unimpressive in themselves, and yet they are seen as good works in the sight of God because of our relationship to him. A non-Christian, who is not part of the Church of God, can not do any good works in the sight of God. We are assured that *"Without faith it is impossible to please Him."* (Hebrews 11:6). This can only mean that, even though an unbeliever does exactly the same as the Christian, yet, because he does not have faith, it is not a good work pleasing to God, in the same sense as when the Christian does it. From this it is evident that ultimately it is our relationship to God that makes all the difference. If we are Christians who have faith, our

---

[35] cp.Luke 21:1-4

life is full of good works, but if we are not Christians we can't do any good works at all.[36] So it is in the relationship between a man and his wife too. When a husband loves his wife as Christ loved the Church, then virtually everything that she does (unless it is in rebellion against him) is treasured by him. That is probably why some have said that love is blind. It fails to see the faults of the other person and sees everything as good, simply because she is his beloved. But this is a very important part of true love. We should not deplore it. Because of their life together, the husband sees the simple things that his wife does as good and special to him. It is therefore finally who she is, rather than what she does, that matters most and makes her so dear to her husband. She will never be perfect, but she is held dear by him because of whom she is, and he needs to reassure her of this often. His love for her needs to make her delighted that she is truly feminine, that she is precious to him, and that she is his wife. This is the nature also of Christ's love for his Church. Because of it we are glad to be Christians and belong to him.

CHRIST IS THE SPIRITUAL LEADER OF HIS CHURCH

Few things could be more obvious to the Christian than that Christ is the spiritual leader of his Church. It was Christ who led his Church in every way spiritually. He is her spiritual prophet, priest and king. As her prophet, Christ is the teacher of his Church. Not only did he teach his disciples and others when he was on earth, as one having authority,[37] but his Word is to be the guide and rule for his Church for all time. This is so when he sends out his apostles and pastors to proclaim his word. It is not to be their own word that is proclaimed to the Church, but the Word of Christ her Lord. He is the teaching authority for his Church. He specifically says to his disciples, *"He that heareth you heareth me; and he that despiseth you despiseth me; and he that despiseth me despiseth him that sent me."* (Luke 10:16). As the priest of his Church he also took it upon himself to fulfil the law perfectly on her behalf. Just as the Old Testament priests were responsible for the fulfilment of the ceremonial law, so Christ has fulfilled the law for his Church too. Just as the ancient priests offered up the sacrifices in the temple for the sins of the people, so Christ offered up himself as the one great sacrifice for the sins of the world. This priestly act brought to fulfilment all other priestly sacrifices and gave them meaning. As the priests prayed for the

---

[36] cp. Heb. 11:6
[37] cp. Matt. 7:29

people before the altar of incense, so Christ still intercedes for his Church before the throne of God. He is also the true spiritual king of his church who rules over her here in this world and will finally rule as King of kings for all eternity. In every respect Christ is the spiritual leader of his Church. This is not for his benefit but for her own good and blessing.

From this it should be obvious that the husband is to be the spiritual leader and spokesman for his wife and family. He is to be the teacher and lead in their reading and study of God's Word. As a prophet he should take the lead in their family worship, reading from the Scriptures or from other devotional material for the spiritual nourishment of his wife and family. He should lead them in prayer, and be their spiritual spokesman before the world. He should make the spiritual decisions of the family, and see to it that they are all regularly at worship in the house of God whenever services are held. He should lead them spiritually by word and example. He is the one who must finally give an account to God for how he fulfilled this role, and therefore he is to do this with a deep sense of responsibility. This implies that he is to provide spiritual food and drink not only for his wife, at her level, but for each one of his children at their level. This means that he will see to it that he finds suitable devotional material for the various age groups in his family and will provide for them in such a way that they do not remain spiritually stunted but grow and mature spiritually. For all these things the Lord holds him primarily responsible.

This is not to say that the wife may not also read the Word of God and other devotional material in the family under the leadership of her husband, especially when he is away or unable to lead in person. But it means that it will at all times be recognised that he is to be the prophet and priest in their relationship. Where these roles are reversed, and the wife is seen as the spiritual leader of the household, as, for instance, when the wife is a Christian but the husband is not, and he simply suffers through the process but takes no interest in it, let alone any leadership role, there is bound to be a serious weakness. Not so much, possibly, in the case of the wife, who understands that this is an irregular, emergency situation, and not how it ought to be, but if there are children, this will very likely result in an attitude which regards all religion and religious exercises as the business of women. As they grow into men, the boys will probably stay away from worship, and leave any responsibilities in the church to their wives. Feminine leadership in the church almost always results in an abdication of male responsibility. When that happens it is only one generation from disintegration. Those who are pushing

47

for women to take positions of leadership in worship, not only in the home but in the public worship of the congregation, are sowing poison seed which will be reaped by a future generation and may well at first leave their churches empty of men, and then later of women, to be filled instead by tyres or some other warehouse goods. We can not abandon the model of the Christ/Church relationship, let alone reverse roles, without very serious consequences.

CHRIST'S FORGIVENESS AND PATIENCE

One outstanding quality of Christ's love for his Church was his patient long-suffering and forgiveness to her. Even though he forgave her initially, yet she continues to sin against him daily. He sets no time limits for her to bring herself up to standard, and put away all evil. Nor does he allow her a limited number of transgressions of the same nature before he refuses to forgive and resorts to revenge. He is simply long- suffering and ready to forgive as often as that is necessary.[38] That is also to be the nature of a husband's love for his wife. He must train himself to show that long-suffering nature of Christ to his wife. This may not be easy for most men, especially those who are very busy or under pressure. One of the most painful experiences in the married life of the author, who is naturally inclined to be impatient, and who took a pride in being on time, was to have to learn to be patient with a wife who seemed to have a different understanding of time, and sometimes made him a little late. After years of training he is still not confident that he has sufficiently learned the patience and long-suffering that Christ would see in us.

It is easy for a man, insulted by his wife's failure or oft recurring fault, to lose patience with her, to blurt out some insult or criticism, and to plan a little act of revenge to teach her a lesson and get her to put away her fault. But that was not the way of Christ the heavenly Bridegroom, and that dare not be the way of loving husbands either. The more a man loses patience with his wife, and raises his voice in resentment, the less she will be able to trust him and commit herself fully to him. That price is far too high to pay for such a lesson. The very fact that a wife knows that something of her conduct aggravates her husband, but can see that he is not allowing this to destroy his patience with her or his forgiveness, will lead her to deeper trust and to greater efforts in trying to please him, and to overcome her faults. Such long suffering forgiveness is a necessary quality of a husband's love if he is to function as the head of his wife.

---

[38] cp. Matt. 18:21f.

48

CHRIST'S TENDERNESS

It should be obvious from the Christ/Church relationship that in all his dealings with her, especially in the exercise of his authority or headship, Christ always deals with her with a special tenderness and understanding. There is never any riding roughshod over his Bride or attempting to force her to do his will. It is true that Christ as head of his Church is uncompromising and absolutely insistent upon his truth. That is the reason why it was necessary for him to give his life for his Church. God's perfect justice could not be compromised. But in all his insistence upon the truth, he is at the same time filled with gentleness and kindness in dealing with his Church. He invites her most tenderly: *"Come unto me all ye that labour and are heavy laden, and I will give you rest."* He pleads with those afraid of being oppressed, *"Take my yoke upon you, and learn of me; for I am meek and lowly in heart: and ye shall find rest for your souls. For my yoke is easy, and my burden is light."* (Matthew 11:28-30). In this sense Christ deals with his Church like a kind and tender-hearted physician, who may have to perform painful procedures and operations for her well-being, but always does so with the utmost kindness and sympathetic tenderness. So the loving husband too, always deals with his beloved with a sense of deep compassion and tenderness. If he must assert his headship for her benefit and blessing, even requiring what to her might be painful and disconcerting, he will, like Christ his Lord, seek to do so with the utmost tenderness and compassion. It is largely this tenderness and understanding concern for his wife in all things, that enables her to entrust herself to him with absolute confidence. This is one of the fine arts of loving, Christian headship – to be able to temper authority with tenderness.

CHRIST DELIGHTS IN HIS CHURCH

Despite the fact that all men are sinners and that Christ hates all sin, yet because Christ has redeemed and sanctified his Church, purifying and perfecting her for himself, the Bible tells us that Christ actually delights in his Church. He is said not only to nourish but to cherish his Church. The original Greek word means to cherish with tender love and care. This is further emphasised by other passages of Scripture which tell us that God actually takes pleasure in his people whom he has sanctified for himself. In Proverbs 11:20 we are told that *"such as are upright in their way are his delight."* And again, *"they that deal truly are his delight."* (Proverbs 12:22).[39] Those who were sinners and incurred the wrath of God, now, through Christ's love and work, have become the objects of God's delight so that he actually adores them.

So the husband, who is filled with the love of Christ, will also delight in and adore his wife. This was the obvious will and intention of God in designing woman for man as he did. Her very form, her figure and feminine nature are to be the source of man's delight and adoration. Whether women realise it or not – and it sometimes seems that many don't, or at least pretend that they don't – woman is designed by God, in form and nature, to be the most beautiful creature in all of creation. She was the climax of God's creation not only in point of time, but, at least as far as man is concerned, in charm and splendour, elegance and grace, beauty and glory. There is no other creature so pleasing to man.

While it is clearly evil for a husband to be obsessed with or dote upon other women, the Lord has ordained that he should adore his wife and lavish his affections upon her. Solomon says, by inspiration, *"Drink water from your own cistern, and running water from your own well. Should your fountains be dispersed abroad, streams of water in the streets? Let them be only your own, and not for strangers with you. Let your fountain be blessed, and rejoice with the wife of your youth. As a loving deer and a graceful doe, let her breasts satisfy you at all times; and always be enraptured with her love. For why should you, my son, be enraptured by an immoral woman, and be embraced in the arms of a seductress?* (Proverbs 5:15-20 RAV).

It is clearly God's will, therefore, that a loving husband is to appreciate his wife, cherishing her as his most charming counterpart. This adoration will express itself not only in dressing his wife in the most beautiful and attractive clothes that enhance her feminine form, but also, according to Solomon, in undressing her and admiring her as she was designed for him by God in the Garden of Eden.

Anyone who has read the Song of Solomon can not but be impressed by the beautiful way in which a husband is fascinated by every feature of his wife. He says to his beloved, *"How beautiful are your feet in sandals, O prince's daughter! The curves of your thighs are like jewels, the work of the hands of a skilful workman. Your navel is a rounded goblet which lacks no blended beverage. Your waist is a heap of wheat set about with lilies. Your two breasts are like two fawns, twins of a gazelle. Your neck is like an ivory tower, your eyes are like the pools of Heshbon by the gate of Bath Rabbim. Your nose is like the tower of Lebanon which looks*

---

[39] cp. also Jer. 9:24

toward Damascus. Your head crowns you like Mount Carmel, and the hair of your head is like purple; the king is held captive by its tresses. (Song of Solomon 7:1-5 RAV). What God has created for man dare not remain unappreciated or its glory remain unsung. Furthermore to know that she is the subject of her husband's ecstasy, will give a mature wife a sense of meaning and fulfilment that is so vital for her emotional stability and well being.

The fact that women are designed to be attractive to men is, of course, the reason why women are used so widely in advertising today. A product that is associated with a beautiful woman will attract more attention than if it were exhibited alone. But the question needs to be asked, to what extent should woman's natural beauty and charm be exploited for such economic advantage?

The Bible clearly indicates that within marriage man is to delight in womanin everything about her but she is not to be exposed and exhibited indiscriminately for the general pleasure of men. There are clearly limits beyond which man's interest in woman, outside of marriage, becomes sinful lust and is condemned by our Lord.[40] To exploit women in this way for advertising is clearly wrong. Within marriage, on the other hand, a husband dare not simply take his wife for granted, but needs to express his pleasure in her as a precious gift of God. He needs to take her into his arms and admire her femininity, compliment her and let her know that she is most appreciated that she is the source of his greatest delight. He will do well to learn of Solomon also to become a little poetic and ecstatic in expressing his admiration for his wife. This is worth more to her than flowers. Her response in devotion and self-surrender will amply reward his efforts.

Perhaps it may not be amiss to point out for the comfort of some ageing women, that husbands have the ability to see their wives not as they appear to others, but according to the image which they have set up in their minds. An aged wife may see herself as most unattractive, because of her wrinkles and other blemishes, but her husband, who knew her in her most glamorous years, will still be able to see her as beautiful through the coloured glasses of his memories. He can still be deeply satisfied in her though others see her simply as an old lady. Though she may have lost her youthful glamour, she is still his complement, and her feminine nature and self-surrendering love make her most precious to him so that he will not cease to love and admire her. This, of course, is how Christ sees his Bride. Though she is far from holy and righteous in herself, he sees her as holy and without blemish because of her relationship to him. And so he holds her in esteem despite her present imperfections.

---

[40] cp. Matt. 5:27-28

It is surely part of the sacrificial love that a husband should have for his wife, that he forsakes all others and gives himself to her only. Of course, in the Christ/Church relationship, there is only one Church in the sense of the communion of saints, or the whole number of believers in Christ, and so there is no question of Christ giving himself to any other Bride. This is how it is to be in marriage also. This is one of the requirements or prerequisites of marriage, and has been so right from the beginning.[41] Any failure to give himself completely to his wife alone, is finally a rejection of marriage itself. It is the one scriptural cause for divorce. Jesus says, *"Whosoever shall put away his wife, except it be for fornication, and shall marry another, committeth adultery."* (Matthew 19:9).

Unfortunately there are many men, who, while not openly breaking their marriage relationship by committing fornication with some other woman, nevertheless do not forsake all others as far as their interests are concerned. They dote on other women, possibly even film stars or TV personnel in such a way that this detracts from their devotion to their own wife. They may even make unfavourable comments to her, comparing her with the stars of their fancy. Of course there may be numerous other women who are more beautiful, and who have a lovelier personality than their wife. A husband is not blind to this nor insensitive, but he knows that God has given him his wife, and she is the one to whom he must devote all his affection and attention, and he will not undermine their life together by any sort of unfavourable comments or comparisons. This too is part of the nature of the love of Christ for his Church.

This does not mean that there is no place for the appreciation of other women and their role in life. Far from it, women have a very important role and function for man not only in marriage, but in society generally. Their very femininity, in fact their very presence, especially in areas where they have special qualities and graces, is of vital importance for man. One word of encouragement, or even a smile from a sympathetic and truly feminine lady may do more for a man than reason can explain. Without any sexual connotations, pure femininity is a necessary part of a man's environment. It enables him to be and to perform at his best — to act and live out his role as a man, with dignity and responsibility. It is finally in his relationship with women that a man will be most manly. Unless she, by her presence, provides him with the opportunity and challenge to be truly masculine and manly,

---

[41] cp. Gen. 2:24

he will find less urge to be so, and will fail to be what he was created to be. Her very presence, therefore – being what she is – is vital not only within marriage but in society generally.

From all of this we can see that for a husband to be the head of his wife, means to bestow his honour upon her, and to see her as his ultimate glory. For any woman to covet this awesome role of man and want to be head in place of her husband is to empty herself of everything that it means to be a woman. It finally means to hate herself and everything that tends to her glory. But for a husband to decline this awesome role of headship in his life with his wife is to fail to qualify for the title "man". It is a confession of complete immaturity at best, or of hopeless failure to be what he was designed to be.

Every husband will fail in numerous ways to be the sort of head that God designed him to be, but at least, if he wants to enter that divine institution of marriage, he should be ready to make it a matter of careful study, earnest prayer and vigorous endeavour to be what he was intended to be. Even imperfect and faulty efforts to follow the example of Christ will be most richly rewarded.

Chapter 6

THE WIFE
AS THE GLORY OF HER HUSBAND

There are only two simple statements by St. Paul in the Ephesians passage addressed to wives. *"Wives, be subject to your husbands, as to the Lord, for the husband is the head of the wife, even as Christ is the head of the church,"* and *"As the church is subject to Christ, so let wives also be subject in everything to their husbands."* (Ephesians 5:22, 24). The one requirement of the wife to her husband mentioned here is submission in everything, like the Church is subject to Christ. Amazing! The wife is not even told to love her husband, but only to submit to him. Surely love would have to be one of the most important requirements of a wife for her husband if they are going to be happy. Has the apostle Paul really failed so badly to understand marriage that he does not even require wives to love their husbands? This troubled the author for years. While he was aware of a number of passages in the Bible in which husbands are required to love their wives, he could find only one passage where the wife is actually told to love her husband.[42] On the other hand there are many passages which require a wife to submit to her husband or to be subject to him, but surely love is more important than submission?

Finally he saw that the Holy Spirit, speaking through St. Paul, understood far more about marriage and love than he did. It dawned on him that St. Paul understood that the nature of a woman's love for her husband is different from the love of a husband for his wife. While a man's love is characterised by outgoing, self-sacrificing commitment and responsibility, a woman's love is characterised rather by submission in all things to her husband, just as St. Paul says. This is what it means for a woman to love her husband.

Many people, who talk most about love, have very little idea of what it really is. They think of it as some elated feeling that sweeps them on to cloud nine. But really it is something much more fundamental than that. It is both a form of surrender and victory at the same time. It gives everything and receives everything. It says with Solomon, *"I am my beloved's and my beloved is mine."* Anything short of that is ultimately nothing but affection mixed with selfishness. True love is a serious thing indeed. It is a complete commitment that knows no half measures. This

---

[42] cp. Tit. 2:4

54

is so both in masculine love as well as in feminine love. The difference being, not one of degree, but of direction, as it were. Masculine love is more out-going or active, more giving, while feminine love more passive or receptive. The essential difference between masculine and feminine love is the difference between self-sacrifice, and self-surrender. Man's love as head sacrifices himself for his beloved. Woman's love surrenders herself for the beloved. Paul calls it being submissive to her husband. Only such love is a true foundation for marriage.

THE CHURCH IS SUBMISSIVE TO CHRIST

What is required of the wife in being submissive in all things to her husband is therefore simply that she love him with that submissive, feminine love, as the Church is subject to Christ. This is not an unqualified subjection, as some might like to think, but it is clearly qualified by two expressions, *"as to the Lord,"* and *"as the church is subject to Christ."* In such a way the wife is to be subject in all things to her husband. This is a very profound commitment indeed. It is not something that she can play at, or decide to limit in some way with varying degrees from time to time in various circumstances.

For the wife to be subject to her husband as unto the Lord, means that she will be subject to him because, and in as much as, he exercises the authority of the Lord. This does not make the husband more important than his wife, or in any way suggest that he is better in God's sight, it simply acknowledges the ordinance of God's authority, and humbly accepts the different roles that he has instituted.

In other words, in the institution which God has given, where the husband truly treats his wife like Christ treats his Church, there the wife will be able to submit herself to her husband fully and completely in all things, with the utmost trust and confidence, just like the Church is subject to Christ. If there is any hesitation whatever, on the part of the wife to submit herself completely to her husband, this is a clear indication, either that the husband has failed to show that self-sacrificing love for her that Christ showed to his Church, and that therefore he is in need of help in this vital matter, or that she has failed to understand the true nature of marriage. After a period of courtship in which a couple have come to know each other very closely, and they have both come to understand how God wants them to live in marriage, there should be no hesitation whatsoever for the wife to submit herself fully and completely into the loving hands of him who will represent God to her.

This, of course, is the way in which the Church is subject to Christ. She subjects herself to Christ her heavenly Bridegroom simply because she is assured of his great self-sacrificing love for her, his complete responsibility, his full commitment to do all things for her benefit and blessing, his determination to rule the entire world for her advantage. The Church is ready to submit to the headship and leadership of Christ her Lord even when this means suffering and persecution, simply because of the absolute faithfulness and benevolence of Christ her Lord. Even if her husband's calling or his faithfulness to God should bring hardship and suffering upon her, his self-sacrifice for her, and his absolute commitment to her welfare, will allow her to give herself to him in complete confidence even in times of trouble.

Clearly all of this presupposes and depends upon the proper love of the husband for his wife. Without this love such subjection becomes impossible or very risky. That is why the marriage vow is a very serious matter and should be made only when couples are certain that they have reached such a degree of understanding and love that they can commit themselves to each other for life with absolute confidence. That is also why de facto relationships in which couples are not prepared to make such a lifelong commitment to each other are simply a mockery of the institution of marriage. A man who does not have such a love for his girlfriend, that he is ready to sacrifice all for her, give himself completely for her, and take the full responsibility for her no matter what, is not acting like Christ. Instead of being like the Good Shepherd who gives his life for the sheep, he is like the wretched hireling, who is there only to use them for his advantage. Such a hireling can not expect his partner to give herself to him in proper submission. He has given her no ground or basis for such trust and confidence. And so neither party can live as God intended for them. Their relationship becomes a mockery and abuse of God's institution. It is the result of a failure to understand what marriage is all about. They see it simply as a human contract. This is a recipe for disaster.

Perhaps we should be reminded that while the wife is required to submit herself to her husband, as to her head, yet, as we saw before, this will redound to her ultimate glory. In Christ's order things happen differently than they do in the political world. The way in which the world seeks to gain honour and glory is usually by pushing one's-self forward, and grabbing whatever power and authority he can, certainly not by submission to some other authority or power. The poor, deluded world does not seem to know any other way of attaining recognition or glory. This is the reason for the ruthless power struggle that we see all about us in the world. This is the way that misguided feminists seek after glory, but this is not the way that the Church is glorified, nor that woman will attain to true glory and eminence in her relationship with man. The reason for this lies in the unalterable fact that woman was created to be the complementary counterpart to man. Her glory will be realised in a way opposite to that of man. A failure to realise this and to understand this basic truth has led many to become very disillusioned and disappointed in life. Why is it that men are usually taller than women, and that women generally appear more beautiful looking up than looking down? Could such things be pointers to the god-ordained relationship between husband and wife? They may certainly provide food for thought.

It seems to be a fact, demonstrated statistically, that many women who have spent years at colleges and universities, and who may graduate with honours, and possibly take on some prestigious job, finally never get married, even though they may dearly want to do so. Why should it be that those who seem to have so much to recommend them finally are not chosen in marriage, while their much less qualified sisters are happily married? Some have suggested that the high qualifications of such women may tend to scare men off. This may sound plausible, but it is most probably not the true reason at all. There would be at least as many men who are well qualified to marry such learned women, and who would have no reason to fear their qualifications. And yet these women are not chosen in marriage. It is more likely that something has happened in the process of their becoming highly educated and qualified academically which spoils their chances of marriage. Other things being equal, it would seem that this finally has got to be related to what man needs and looks for in a wife. It has got to be related to a woman's willingness to give herself to a man in self-surrendering love. In some subtle way this charming feminine quality has probably been compromised or reduced, so that, while man generally may respect her, yet she does not appeal to him as a wife. Ultimately man can not give himself to a woman with the sort of self-sacrificing love required in marriage, unless she is ready to show those submissive qualities that St. Paul points to in Ephesians 5. The exercise of power and authority and academic prestige, so often undermines a woman's truly feminine nature. She would be far more appreciated if she learned to excel in that amazing passive power which is made perfect in weakness.

THE CHURCH TAKES CHRIST'S NAME

The relationship between Christ and his Church, in the heavenly marriage, is signed and sealed by the Church taking upon herself the name of Christ her Bridegroom. Every member of the Church is baptised into the name of Christ. The baptised person is then given a Christian name, in the original understanding of that term, to indicate his true identity. His surname (sire name) was received from his earthly father, and indicated his physical ancestry and relationship. His Christian name was given to him to indicate his spiritual relationship. In our modern times Christian names have lost their significance and everyone is thought to have a Christian name, even those who are not Christians. Recently, in our increasingly secular age that wishes to dispense with any Christian associations, the Christian name is now called a "given name".

Not only the individual member of the Church, but the Church itself takes the name of Christ her Lord, and is well called the "Christian Church". This is no accident. Even though the name "Christian" may first have been given by men,[43] it truthfully indicates their proper relationship. The Church is called Christian because Christ is her head and she belongs to him as her Lord.

In a similar way, if our marriage is to follow the pattern of Christ and the Church, the wife is to take on the name of her husband. A scriptural marriage is not made up of two separate individuals living together in some contractual relationship, but it is a unity. Jesus assures us that they are no longer two, but one flesh.[44] If they are no longer two, but one, it is only proper that they bear a common name. Since the husband is the head of the wife and must take the final responsibility for their relationship, it is fitting that the wife should bear the name of her husband. This was instituted by God right from the very beginning in the Garden of Eden. We read in Genesis 5:2 that the man and his wife bore the name of the man, "Adam", "*in the likeness of God made he him; Male and female created he them; and blessed them, and called their name Adam, in the day when they were created.*" Not only Adam was called Adam (man), but Eve too bore the name of her husband Adam.

The refusal of many modern women to bear the name of their husband, and to retain their so-called maiden name (actually the surname of their father), is not an insignificant detail, but it is really a rebellion first against the requirement of Scripture for a wife to seek the honour of her husband by acknowledging his headship and submitting herself to him, as well as a rebellion against the whole scriptural concept of marriage. While those who make such demands may do so out of a shallow lack of un-

---

[43] cp Rom. 11:26
[44] cp Matt. 19:6

derstanding of what they are in fact doing, yet those who are capable of a little deeper insight will see that, however trivial this may appear, it is nevertheless most significant. It reveals the true spirit of those who advocate it, in that it rejects the entire Christ/Church relationship in marriage – the very basis of a truly biblical relationship. It is a refusal to accord the husband the honour of headship and is a desecration of the divine archetype of marriage.

It might not be amiss also to notice in passing, that when God called the male and female persons whom he had created, "Adam", there was no special limitation of this term to a married couple, but to male and female human beings generally. *Male and female created he them; and blessed them, and called their name Adam, in the day when they were created."* (Genesis 5:2). This would indicate that the so-called sexist terminology, referring to man and woman together by the generic term "man" is ordained by God. The revolt against using such masculine terms for the human race is therefore not an insignificant triviality. It is ultimately a revolt against what God himself has instituted. Of course it is understandable that a society which refuses to acknowledge the original creation of man and woman in the image and glory of God, and sees them as nothing but a development from apelike ancestors, may rejoice when even their language becomes more and more divorced from any spiritual relationship with their Creator, and espouses their supposed animal ancestry. However, the extent to which popular prejudice, is successful in eliminating all sexist terminology from our language and also from the Bible, will be a reflection of the degree to which our generation has impoverished itself by surrendering the honour and dignity that God bestowed on his creation in the beginning, making man and woman an earthly picture of the heavenly relationship between Christ and his Church.

THE CHURCH IS JUSTIFIED BY CHRIST

To be justified, in the proper biblical sense, means not to **become** holy and righteous, but to **be declared** holy and righteous, on account of what Christ has done for us. The Christian retains his sinful nature, so that he still falls into sin again and again, as even St. Paul had to confess,[45] and yet he is justified before God in the sense that his sins are forgiven and he is declared to be just and righteous. Justification is an act of God, not of man. It is a declaration by the eternal Judge that the sinner is acquitted or pronounced not guilty of the charges brought against him. It is

---

[45] cp Rom. 7:19

in this way that the Church is justified by Christ. This is very vividly portrayed in Zechariah 3, where the Church is portrayed as Joshua the high priest, standing before the Lord, clothed in filthy garments, and Satan standing at his right hand to accuse him. But the Lord, the eternal Judge, rebukes Satan and commands that Joshua's filthy garment should be taken away from him, and says, *"Behold, I have caused thine iniquity to pass from thee, and I will clothe thee with change of raiment."* [46] So the Church is justified in the sense that her sins are taken away and she is clothed with the righteousness of Christ. In other words her righteousness is not her own, but it is provided for her by Christ. It is a righteousness which exceeds the righteousness of the Scribes and Pharisees,[47] so that she is justified before God.

In a similar way, a wife is to be adorned with the clothes that her husband provides for her. She is to be dressed in the clothes which he sees as beautiful and glorious. They are to have the effect of making her attractive in his sight. As in justification, the purpose is not to make the Church appear justified before the world, or in her own sight, but in the sight of God, so in the case of woman, the purpose of her clothing and adornment is not to make her appealing in the eyes of the world, or even in her own estimation, but in the eyes of her husband. In this way she becomes most delightful to him, and that is what matters. Just as the sinner does not become perfect in himself, but retains his old sinful nature, and is nevertheless justified before God, so the wife does not become perfect in herself — without spot or wrinkle or any such thing — but, when she allows herself to be dressed by her husband, she is nevertheless seen by him as beautiful and glorious.

This may seem somewhat hard and inconsiderate to an immature and inexperienced wife, who has some very definite ideas about what sort of clothes she will wear and how she wants to look, but it will not take her long to find out that unless she is very sensitive to her husband's likes and dislikes she could destroy his affection toward her, and ruin their relationship. Like the self-righteousness of the Pharisees could not justify them before God, so the self-chosen adornment of a head-strong, independent wife, will not win the heart of her husband either. The sooner she learns to be guided in her dress by what pleases him, the sooner she will be freed from the tears of disappointment and experience the thrill of being the delight and glory of the one who matters most in her life.

---

[46] cp Zech. 3:4

[47] cp Matt. 5:20

Perhaps a wife, on being told that she should be subject to her husband as the Church is subject to Christ, might be tempted to think to herself that that is all right for the Church, because Christ her Lord is perfect in every way. Her husband, on the other hand, is a sinful mortal who is full of faults and imperfections. How can she subject herself to him with any sort of confidence? She is probably aware of a number of his weaknesses and imperfections. Is it all right for her to hope, and perhaps secretly plan, to change him to suit herself?

First of all it should be obvious that there may well be faults and imperfections in a man that a given woman simply can not live with. But this was the purpose of their courtship, to get to know each other, and find out if there were any such weaknesses and blots in each other's character or personality, that make it impossible for them to live together. If so they should have broken off their relationship, and not gone into marriage with the secret hope that things might still work out, or that in some way they might be able to change their partner. And so if a couple is married by their own choice, one should be able to assume that there are no imperfections or blots in their character that would make it absolutely impossible for them to live together happily.

Given this, it must be said that, basically a wife must accept her husband for what he is, just as the Church accepts Christ her Lord for what he is. The Church can not and dare not try to change Christ her Lord, but must accept him for what he is and learn to love him so. Any scheming or plotting on the part of the Church to change Christ would be a rejection of him – a falling away. Even Christ accepts us just as we are, with all our imperfections, whether we will change much in this life or not, and we must accept him just as he is. One of the most dangerous things that a wife can do is actively to set about trying to change her husband to suit herself. He will immediately sense that she has not really accepted him for what he is, and he will take this as rejection. If she nags him with respect to his faults, be it smoking, or failing to help her with the dishes or whatever, he will most probably resist her attacks, first by sharp remarks, and then by clamming up, and perhaps even by making himself scarce, keeping out of her way in the pub with his mates or wherever.[48] This is courting disaster. Before she knows it she will find herself estranged from the man who seemed to offer such promises of joy and satisfaction in her life.

The problem is simply that, by not accepting him as he is, his wife has made him feel that his position as head and leader of the

---

[48] cp Prov. 25:24

household is being threatened or rejected. Every man knows that he is not perfect and is not so naive as to think that his wife will not notice his numerous faults. He will not even mind discussing them with her. But, because of his position and responsibility, he will not accept a challenge to his authority. He will meet force with force if necessary, and show who is boss. Still worse he may even abdicate his position, and leave everything to his wife, and then delight in fouling things up for her as she tries to wear his pants. Seemingly victorious, she will go through life despised and resented, and he will find ways of keeping out of her way, possibly even with another woman. In trying to improve her husband she has destroyed their marriage and blown everything.

The trouble was that she used the wrong kind of power to accomplish what might have been a praiseworthy aim. She stood up to him and usurped his power, triggering a direct confrontation in which she had to be the ultimate looser. Had she used that power that the Lord has given her, the paradoxical power of feminine submission, the outcome would have been quite different. This is one power for which a man has no counter. Instead of physical threats and demonstrations of authority against her humble submission, he can be moved only to amazement and wonder, to respect, to love, to glorify and to embrace his wife. With her gentleness, and submission, with a truly feminine attitude and look, she can do more to influence him than in any other way. This is a power by which he ultimately delights to be conquered. This is how the apostle Peter urges Christian wives married to unbelieving partners, to deal with their husbands. He says, *"Likewise, ye wives, be in subjection to your own husbands; that, if any obey not the word, they also may without the word be won by the conversation of the wives; while they behold your chaste conversation coupled with fear."* (I Peter 3:1-2).

By her whole manner, her speech, and her actions a wife must let her husband feel that she accepts him as her leader and head, and will always submit to him. Even if there are things about him that could and should be improved, she will still submit to him and affirm his leadership. Without this she can accomplish nothing, but will only destroy their marriage. By her very femininity, by her submissive love, he will be moved to excel himself in expressions of love for her too. Changes that she could never effect by nagging, or by forceful demands, may come simply as a wonderful bonus in response to her feminine, submissive love.

THE CHURCH TRUSTS HER LORD

One of the most natural qualities of the Church is that she has come to trust her Lord. Trust is a part of true faith, without which we can have no saving relationship with Christ at all, and this trust is expressed in a confident, cheerful resignation and commitment to Christ. Jesus enjoins such trust upon us when he says in Matthew 7:31, *"Take no thought, saying, what shall we eat? or, What shall we drink? or, Wherewithal shall we be clothed?"* The Christian is not to be filled with anxious care or worry about the things of this life, simply because his heavenly Father knows that he has need of these things, and will therefore take good care of them all. He can simply live in cheerful contentment, trusting in the Lord to provide for him.

This is true also with respect to all other things, including a concern for the problems of life, the hatred of the world and our own sinfulness. The Lord admonishes us to cast all our care upon him for he careth for us.[49] And Jesus invites us all with comforting assurance, *"Come unto me, all ye that labour and are heavy laden, and I will give you rest."*[50] Quite obviously he wants his Christians to have a happy confidence and a sense of pleasant security in him, so that they can be relaxed and happy in his presence, and not be given to cares and worry. This is stressed in numerous places also in the Psalms. For instance in Psalm 127:2 we are told, *"It is vain for you to rise up early, to sit up late, to eat the bread of sorrows: for so he giveth his beloved sleep."* The Christian is simply to look to Christ with cheerful trust and confidence.

The same is true in the relationship between husband and wife. The wife is to have such a trusting confidence in her husband and his loving care and concern for her that she can relax in blissful peace and joy in his presence. This trust will show itself in pleasant smiles and a cheerful disposition, which is so delightful to a loving husband. No husband wants to see his wife constantly frowning and dejected. Not only does this make her sour and unattractive to him, but it hurts him at least as much as it hurts her. She should not need to be worried or concerned, either about her own welfare, or about her relationship to him, but simply be able to relax in carefree pleasantness.

A husband whose wife is always glum and does not smile cheerfully, needs to ask himself whether he has perhaps failed her very seriously, in that he has not given her sufficient grounds for trust and confidence. No wife will be able to maintain a smiling, cheerful disposition if this is the case. On the other hand, for a wife

---

[49] cp I Pet. 5:7

[50] cp Matt. 11:28

who has every reason to be filled with confidence and trust in her husband, simply to make herself glum and refuse to smile pleasantly, is a declaration that she is refusing to commit herself properly to him. This will hurt her husband – it may possibly be deliberately intended to do so – but it will harm her most of all. There is nothing so conducive of sickness or depression, and the ageing process, as a frowning, angry, and bitter disposition. A wife who wants to punish her husband with such an attitude, will not only punish him very effectively and possibly also destroy his love for her, but will also destroy herself in the process. On the other hand there is nothing quite so uplifting and healing, either for man or woman, as a pleasant disposition and the welcome smile of a loving wife. This radiates a grace and charm which inspires man to be and to give of his best.

A cheerful, smiling disposition is probably also the most effective beauty treatment that any woman can have. All the cosmetics in the world will be utterly lost and to no effect on the face of a frowning, bitter woman. On the other hand a cheerful, smiling disposition, even without any make up, will tend to develop a charming and delightful face that will not only satisfy a woman herself, but will be the pride and joy of her husband. If only women would practice this wonderful therapy more devotedly there would be a lot more beautiful women in the world, as well as happy marriages, even though some cosmetic firms might have to suffer.

THE CHURCH ADMIRES HER LORD

One of the repeated responses of the Church to Christ her Lord is to give praise and honour to him, especially for his great love and the salvation which he has won for us. This should be a clue to wives. They should see it as important therefore to admire, to honour and to praise their husbands. St. Paul says that the wife should see that she reverence her husband.[51] To reverence him surely means to respect, honour, and hold him in esteem. But this reverence or respect is not simply to be a silent condition in her heart, but it needs to be expressed, just as we express praise and thanks to Christ. Someone has said, a woman needs to be loved, but a man needs to be admired. One would have thought that they both need to be admired, but for different things. A woman probably needs to be adored most for what she is, for her personal appearance, her grace and charms – simply because she is wonderful. But it should not cease there, she also needs to be

---

[51] cp Eph. 5:33

cherished for the good things that she does. A man, on the other hand, needs to be admired chiefly for what he does, for his accomplishments, his principles and sticking to his convictions. But it is sometimes also of encouragement for him to know that he is treasured for his masculine, physical nature. Such admiration will do more for the relationship between husband and wife than they may expect. If the wife lets it be seen that she has a high opinion of her husband, and says so, she will be the one who is most rewarded. Such expressions of appreciation will undoubtedly do much to enhance the husband's self-esteem, but in doing so it is bound to remind him of who he is and to trigger off a response of admiration and affection for his wife.

Many marriages become indifferent and may finally disintegrate simply because the partners tend to take each other too much for granted. They don't praise and commend each other. A wife who finds that her husband is spending too much time on the golf course, or that he goes off to be alone by himself, had better not think she will rectify the problem by nagging him into spending more time with her. She needs instead to ask herself, when last did she take any real notice of him, and praise or compliment him for what he does. If he feels that he is not appreciated or treasured for what he does, why should he share his life and feelings with someone who is only bored by him? He will clam up and isolate himself. The end result is tragedy. It is the wife's business – a part of her charm – that she will let her husband know and feel that he is appreciated for what he is and for what he does as her head.

THE CHURCH PERFECTS HERSELF FOR CHRIST

It is one of the concerns of the Church that she will seek to perfect and adorn herself for Christ her Lord. She is not content simply to rejoice in the fact that Christ has forgiven all her sins. Because she belongs to Christ and has come to know what sort of a life pleases him, she seeks to sanctify herself for him, putting away all evil and practicing the righteousness that pleases Christ her Lord.

So the devoted wife too, will not take the attitude that now that she has been accepted by her husband so that they are married, there is no further need for her to make herself attractive to him. She can wear any old clothes in his presence and dress up only when she goes out so as to impress the world. It doesn't matter about her husband; there is no further need to please him. They are safely married.

This is ultimately an insult to her husband, as it would be to Christ, if the Church treated him in this way. He has rather married her and made her his own so that she can appear *"before him in splendour, without spot or wrinkle or any such thing... holy and without blemish,"* as Paul says of the Church. It is her privilege now to dress herself and adorn herself in a way that pleases and delights him. There is probably nothing more uplifting and rewarding for a man than to see his wife radiantly beautiful before him. She is his glory and he wants it that way.

A wife who takes the trouble to present herself in a pleasing manner to her husband will not be disappointed in his response. A loving husband will usually be very quick to let her know that he appreciates every effort on her part to please him. She will be rewarded with just what she needs as he lavishes his affection on her, so that she is pleased to be his wife. On the other hand, the woman who ceases to care how she dresses and presents herself to her husband, need not be surprised if he loses interest in her, and retreats more and more into himself. He is not perfect like Christ is perfect, and his love for his wife will wane if it is not reinforced by appropriate responses from her.

Incidentally, it is a fact that a woman will nearly always be treated by man according to the way she dresses and presents herself. If she dresses in noble, neat attire, she will be treated in a noble manner with appropriate courtesy and attention. If she dresses in a sloppy, indifferent manner, with T shirt and denim jeans, she will be treated in a similar, sloppy and indifferent manner. If she dresses in sexy or tight and revealing clothes, she will be treated in a similar way. The understanding and observant wife can virtually regulate the way she will be treated. By her very appearance she tells her husband how she feels toward him and how she wants to be treated. She has far more power to regulate this than she may realise.

This has some further connotations that it might be worthwhile for modern women, and especially mothers of teenage children to take note of. By taking good care of the way that they dress, and the way their daughters dress, they can probably do far more to regulate the behaviour of the community than by political involvement. Again they have a silent power that may be more effective than all the political punch that some think is so important.

THE CHURCH ADAPTS TO CHRIST

It is surely obvious that the Church needs to adapt herself completely to Christ her Lord. There can be no thought of him adapting himself to suit the Church, as if it were some fifty/fifty arrangement. This is a lesson that every wife needs to learn from the Church too. She must adapt herself to her husband, and not the other way around. This may sound very unfair by modern standards. Surely he ought to adapt himself to her just as much as she to him. But this is not so according to Scripture. The command of the Lord for wives to submit to their husband's leadership is a clear injunction that she must adapt to him and his way of life. If women don't like this and refuse to adapt themselves to man, very well, they have the choice of marrying a man whose way of life suits their own, or of not getting married at all. The option of demanding that their husband adapt to suit their lifestyle is simply not available, as far as the Scriptures are concerned. This might sound cruel to some headstrong girls, but maybe they will live to experience the truth of it, and only wish that they had believed it without the need to experience the pain that results from rejecting this truth in the first place, and jeopardising their marriage.

There is no denying that the life-style of some men is almost impossible for most women to endure. It is a mystery how any woman could be happily married to a sailor who is home for only a few weeks in a year. This seems like an utter abuse of marriage. It is simply asking for trouble. If this is really how it is, one would think that the responsible naval authorities would see to it that such conditions are changed radically. It may be necessary in time of war, but it can hardly be excused in times of peace. With such a system women might just as well be conscripted to become cannon fodder. The reason they are not, is ultimately because they are too important for the stability of the country to be called away from their home, but with such marriage conditions, that stability is undermined any way, so that there is no stability left for them to maintain.

It may not be easy, in many cases, for a woman to adapt to her husband. But once she has married him, for better or for worse, that is what she has undertaken to do. If she does so valiantly, so that her husband can see that she is doing this for his sake, she may be surprised to find that he will make great sacrifices, and possibly important changes to make it easier and better for her. To dig her toes in and refuse to adapt to him, is a course of certain disaster. Even if she does so only occasionally, she will probably bitterly regret it. If he wants to do something special, like go away with her for the weekend, and she wants to stay at home and work in the garden, and in the showdown that ensues, she "wins" and they decide to stay at home, she may find that every minute of that weekend was in fact a pain, and that she could not be happy

67

with her guilty conscience and her offended partner. The gloom that she brought over the household not only for that weekend but for days later, by her refusal to adapt was simply not worth it. She would have been happier to follow his lead.

The worst thing a woman can do for herself is to win an argument against her husband by means of force or threats. That may seem to be what she wants at the time, but the results are always catastrophic. She is the one who will finally be hurt most, as she endures her husband's retreat and watches him abandon her battle-ground to find peace in a safer environment. Instead of ringing her bells she will then begin to wring her hands as she watches her marriage relationship turn sour. No woman can afford to risk taking her husband on with his own kind of weapons. She has the only force that can really conquer him and preserve an honourable peace – the paradoxical power of feminine submission.

THE CHURCH IS FRUITFUL FOR CHRIST

It is most obvious that the Church, as the Bride of Christ, is not to remain sterile and unproductive, but is to be fruitful for Christ her Lord. This was taken for granted from the very beginning. Already before his atoning death and resurrection, when there were only relatively few disciples, Christ sent them out to proclaim his Word and gather others into the kingdom of God. Before his ascension into heaven Christ again gave his disciples the great commission to go out into all the world and make disciples of all nations, *"baptising them in the name of the Father, and of the Son, and of the Holy Ghost: teaching them to observe all things whatsoever I have commanded you."* (Matthew 28:19f.). The church heeded this command and through the preaching of the Word, thousands were soon added to the Church.[52] The apostles and numerous other Christians took the Gospel to all parts of the then-known world so that the Church grew and multiplied greatly. Throughout history the true Church has always been a missionary Church, intent on spreading the Gospel, calling people into the kingdom of God, and nourishing them in the faith.

In a similar way it is God's intention that marriage, is not to be sterile but fruitful in the sense that a couple are to have children, and multiply. Already soon after their creation, the Lord blessed Adam and Eve, and said to them, *"Be fruitful, and multiply, and replenish the earth."* (Genesis 1:28). Just as the Church is to multiply because of her relationship with Christ her Lord, so the wife, because of her relationship with her husband is to be

---

[52] cp Acts 2:41, 47

fruitful and bring forth children. This is to be seen also as a great blessing.[53] The trend of so many modern couples to avoid having children and to regard it as a cross or an affliction is quite unbiblical. Ultimately it is the result of a misguided selfishness. Of course the presence of children in the family limits the freedom of the couple in certain ways, but it also brings great joys and blessings that nothing else can bring. To be a girl is easy enough, if you are born that way. It takes no effort at all, and is certainly no accomplishment. To be truly feminine is a charming art that does take some effort, but is admired by all. To be a successful wife requires special tenderness and loving self-surrender, but is the glory of womanhood. But to be a devoted mother is the ultimate achievement of woman that makes her a blessing that will live in the hearts of her children all their life, and which ultimately shapes the nation. While it does admittedly require effort and patience to be a good mother, this is what we need to become truly mature and understanding people. Children are meant to put us through the mill, and to try us in numerous ways. It is this agitation and friction that finally polishes us to become glorious gems that sparkle and radiate understanding and tenderness. It produces a beauty and glory in woman of the deepest and most lasting nature. It is her family and motherhood that truly perfect a woman and bring her to her ultimate glory, and in doing so also bring true honour to her husband. A woman who has selfishly avoided having children in her most glamorous years, may think she has an advantage, but when she is older, and ceases to be an attraction to those around her, especially if her husband dies, she will find that she has few friends that mean much to her and that life is not rewarding, as she must sit alone in her house, no longer loved and cared about. The mother of a well-managed family, on the other hand, will find that there are new joys, and precious highlights in her life right through to the end, as her children marry, and present her with one grandchild after another. She becomes the dear, understanding and gracious queen mother that is the centre of devotion and admiration for so many.

---

[53] cp Ps. 127:3-5

Chapter 7

A MUTUALLY
SELF-GENERATING RELATIONSHIP

While the husband, as the head of his wife, ought to regard and treat her in accordance with the relationship between Christ and the Church, and while it is true that the wife has no sound basis for complete confidence and trust in her husband unless he does show that sort of love and concern for her, this should not be construed to mean that a wife is to wait for her husband to come up to scratch in his love for her, before she commits herself fully to him. Not only may this in fact never happen in real life, simply because, unlike Christ the heavenly Bridegroom, no man is perfect, but in reality the husband, because of his human weakness, will probably not be able fully to show such love for his wife unless she does commit herself fully to him. In human experience these two are mutually self-generating. One begets the other and the second is born of the first. Each depends upon the other. That is why a period of courtship is necessary for the couple to find out whether such a relationship can be attained and maintained between them.

Some people would maintain that the secret of a successful marriage is to find the right partner. They have suggested that lists of qualities and common interests might be helpful, so that a man should look for some young lady who has the qualities that he desires and sufficient common interests to bind them together. This is a bit like going shopping with a list of things that must be bought. Some people have actually made such lists of qualities that they require in a man or woman who is to be their partner. Whether there is any value in this or not may be debatable. It would appear that the greatest value in such an exercise is to lead them to think about their own set of values, and how important various qualities are. But when it actually comes to choosing a partner it is doubtful whether such a list would even be consulted. It is almost irrelevant. The choice is almost always made on quite different grounds — grounds that are more mystical than rational. It is often not even possible for a couple to say why they chose each other. It is certainly not because the qualities of their partner fitted their shopping list; (they may not fit that list very closely at all); nor because he or she came closest to their ideals. There were probably many others who actually matched their ideals much more closely. Nor is it because the young man thinks

70

his partner to be the most beautiful woman in the world. He knows that she is not, and this does not bother him. He loves her just as she is. Ultimately it is a mystery why a couple choose each other.

But this should not surprise those who are accustomed to be guided by the Christ/Church relationship. It is also a profound mystery why Christ chose us. The Bible assures us that it was not because of anything in us. There was nothing to pick between us. *"There is no difference for all have sinned and come short of the glory of God."* (Romans 3:22f.). And yet God chose his elect.[54] Why? We will never know. This is a mystery that we can not solve. It is not surprising therefore that a man and woman may not be able to explain why they chose each other.

Someone has quite rightly said that marriage is not so much a matter of *choosing* the right person, as *being* the right sort of person. That is no doubt why marriages that are arranged by parents in eastern countries can be very happy. Such partners did not even have a choice, and yet they can be happy, because they learned to be the right sort of people. A man must come to know how to show true love for his wife, and a woman must learn how to show true love for her husband. This is the ultimate secret of success in marriage. It is a mutually self-generating relationship.

From this it should be evident that there dare not be any half measures. Each partner must give himself or herself to their spouse absolutely and completely, with no reserve. Every evidence of some reserve will immediately be seen as a declaration of independence, at least to some degree, and independence is the very antithesis of marriage. While marriage is a unity in one flesh, as Jesus says, *"they are no longer two but one."* (Matthew 19:6 RSV), independence is a refusal to be completely one. That is why every form of independence between partners, is at once seen as a threat to marriage. No matter how unimportant the matter might seem in the estimation of outsiders, yet a partner in marriage can not endure any form of independence without immediately feeling threatened. If he or she notices that there is something that their partner will not share with them, this will at once be seen as a wedge in their relationship, and will serve to undermine true confidence and proper commitment.

For this reason it is obvious to committed Christians that proper unity in marriage is impossible with a partner who is not a Christian, or is of a different faith. If one or both partners of such a marriage take their religion seriously, so that it is a matter

---

[54] cp Eph. 1:3-6; Rom. 8:28-30

[55] cp Matt. 10:37; Lk. 14:26

71

of life and death for them, as Christ requires,[55] then they don't even have this most important aspect of life in common. There is a wedge between them in a most vital area. This is bound to cause serious problems throughout their life. Such obstacles must be faced honestly and resolved before marriage, so that they can enter into marriage without any reservations or areas of independence. A couple is ready for marriage only when they can assert with Ruth, *"Whither thou goest, I will go; and where thou lodgest, I will lodge: thy people shall be my people, and thy God my God: Where thou diest, will I die, and there will I be buried: the Lord do so to me, and more also, if ought but death part thee and me."* (Ruth 1:16-17).

This is true not only in big things, or if one partner wants to go for a holiday alone without the other, perhaps even to a different part of the world, but also if one of them is made to feel that their partner has not fully confided in them, and could well be hiding something. Once married, the days of independence are over, and any suggestion of independence, be it only a failure to answer questions with complete openness or a certain shiftiness in one's glance, will immediately be seen as a wedge to separate them so that they are not truly one and do not wish to be truly one.

For this reason it is necessary for young couples in their courtship to reveal their true selves freely and completely to each other. This includes also their faults and any actions of which they might be justly ashamed. There is often a tendency for partners to hide things from each other, especially bad things about themselves; for fear that their partner may not like them any more if he or she knew what they had done in the past. But this is an illusion. It is rather the other way around. By revealing themselves fully and completely to their partner, and confessing their faults, however shameful, they show that they are serious in committing themselves fully to each other. Far from arousing resentment this actually breeds trust and confidence. On the other hand, if there is something that they withhold from their partner, for fear of arousing distrust, they will, by that very fact, arouse distrust in their partner. To live with a secret that can not be divulged even to the person closest to one's self in life, is bound to result in some form of tension or shiftiness that will finally betray that person, and may even lead to mental problems. It is far better, in fact it is the only honest thing to do, frankly to confess all faults, no matter how painful, and receive the forgiveness of one's partner, and then live in peaceful relaxation in precious oneness and unity.

What if only one partner has shameful confessions to make? It may seem to give the other partner an advantage that could become a sort of leverage point in the future. And so it might seem good stewardship to withhold certain facts until there is a counter confession to balance it. Why should one partner appear more righteous than the other? However, it doesn't work like this. It is not a degree of righteousness or merit that has to be balanced in marriage, but rather a degree of openness and commitment. If one party will not fully expose his or her faults to their partner, for fear of arousing their disgust, because the other did not have similar confessions to make, then there is a bad imbalance which will ultimately make true love impossible. While one partner tries to treat the other with complete frankness and openness, the other retains a reserve or independence which will ultimately undermine mutual trust and commitment.

If one partner does not want to expose all faults fully for fear that he or she might appear inferior in their relationship, they had better take into account that any supposedly better partner who is not ready fully and freely to forgive them, and put this behind them, is not really better after all. In the Christ/Church relationship, it is the Church alone that is the sinner. Christ is absolutely holy and righteous. But the Church does not hesitate to make full and free confession to him, and to do so often, because he is absolutely forgiving. He not only forgives our sins and remembers them no more,[56] but he makes himself responsible for them and bears the guilt of them himself. So the loving husband and wife too, will forgive his or her partner, and because of their unity and oneness, will mutually bear responsibility not only for their future but for their past as well. If a partner is not ready to do this, he or she is not fit for marriage, and it would be better not to marry such a person than to commit themselves to someone with such independence and lack of trust.

There may be all sorts of inequalities between husband and wife, intellectually, socially, financially etc., but there can be no inequalities in the matter of commitment. Because marriage is a unity, both partners must be absolutely committed to each other. Only in such an environment can true love live and grow. It is a mutually dependent relationship.

But of course, in their weakness, both partners may fail in this from time to time. Every failure may indeed come as a blow to their relationship, and may leave a scar that takes time to heal, yet, if they are sincerely committed to developing and perfecting the Christ/Church relationship, that commitment in itself is sufficient basis for hope and assurance that their relationship will be restored, and their marriage will be a great blessing. It is when either party makes it clear that they will not live by the God-ordained marriage principles of the Christ/Church relationship that

---

[56] cp Jer. 31:34

the situation becomes hopeless, and the marriage will degenerate into a humanist/feminist struggle of the survival of the fittest. While the fittest may survive, the marriage will not. At least, if anything of it does survive, it will not be in the sense of that glorious union instituted in the Garden of Eden.

Chapter 8

DOES MARRIAGE AFFECT
THE CHURCH?

Saint Paul writes in Ephesians 5:24ff. *Therefore as the church is subject unto Christ, so let the wives be to their husbands in everything. Husbands love your wives, even as Christ also loved the church, and gave himself for it; that he might sanctify and cleanse it with the washing of water by the word, that he might present it to himself a glorious church, not having spot, or wrinkle, or any such thing; but that it should be holy and without blemish... For this cause shall a man leave his father and mother, and shall be joined unto his wife, and they two shall be one flesh. This is a great mystery: but I speak concerning Christ and the church."* A careful reading of this passage will show that St. Paul does not say simply that we should take the relationship between Christ and his Church as a guide for our marriage. That is a legitimate deduction, expressly implied, but he could well be saying much more than that. He says that there is a mysterious relationship between these two – between Christ and his Church and man and woman in marriage. Would it be right to conclude that this is only a one way process? Could not this mysterious relationship also have implications the other way around, so that the union between husband and wife – be it good or bad – will also tend to affect the Christ/Church relationship? At first sight this may seem ridiculous, if not impossible, and yet it is not ruled out there in Ephesians 5.

We know, of course, that the relationship of Christ to his Church will never vary or alter with the behaviour of man and woman. He is *"the same yesterday, and to day, and for ever."* (Hebrews 13:8), and so he will not act any differently toward his Church no matter how her attitude and behaviour may vary. Perhaps it would be true to say also that the true Church, in the sense of "the communion of saints" (*una sancta*) will also not vary much in her attitude to Christ her Lord. But there may be considerable variation in the attitude and behaviour of individual Christians, or of congregations or of different church organisations from time to time. Is it possible that this attitude and behaviour of the church could in some way be influenced by the prevailing attitude toward marriage in their midst, or by the behaviour of individual couples? In other words, is it possible that the attitude of the church toward Christ, or the way she acts toward him could be to

75

some extent influenced by the way that men and women relate in marriage? To what extent this is possible or even probable is no doubt part of the mystery to which St. Paul refers.

Purely from personal experience the author can testify that in his own case, the more closely he sought to conform the relationship between himself and his wife to that between Christ and his Church, not only the deeper did it become, but the more precious and wonderful did his relationship with Christ become at the same time. The more he perfected his marriage, in conformity with Christ and his Church, the more he came to value his relationship with Christ his Lord. That is to say, to be a Christian — part of the Bride of Christ, came to be ever so much more meaningful, and to be so much richer because of a precious relationship with his wife.

This should not really surprise us. In fact it would be surprising if it were not so. It is difficult to imagine that a couple who have consciously modelled their marriage upon the Christ/Church relationship, and as a result, are enjoying a fulfilling marriage, should then not care to have a good relationship with Christ their Lord. That would be utterly inconsistent. Surely the more they treasure and rejoice in their own marriage, the more they will treasure and rejoice in their relationship with Christ. The one encourages and supports the other. They are reciprocal or mutually self-generating.

It may be easy enough to grant this or even to accept this as being part of the mystery of Christ and his Church to which St. Paul refers, but if this is true, then certain other things follow logically from it which may not be so easy for some to accept. If a conscious effort to model one's marriage on the Christ/Church relationship tends to result in a closer relationship with Christ, so that not only one's marriage, but also the Church benefits from this, then one would expect that the corollary of this would also be true, namely that the less Christian couples conform their marriage to the Christ/Church relationship the remoter their relationship with Christ becomes. While a good marriage among Christians tends to strengthen and support the Church, a bad marriage among Christians will tend to weaken and undermine the Church in her relationship to Christ. While this is not expressly taught, by St. Paul in Ephesians 5, it could well be implied in the mystery of which St. Paul speaks.

There are at least certain areas in which this has been observed to be the case. For instance, where couples have a marriage in which the wife dominates the home, and the husband abdicates from his responsibilities there, it is not surprising that the wife will attempt to take a leading role also in the congregation or church and the husband will abdicate his responsibilities and leave it to the wife. Where there are a number, or even a majority of such marriages in a congregation, or where people have been conditioned to regard these as acceptable, it is not surprising to find that the congregation will also be dominated by women, unless they are prevented from doing so, and the men will abdicate their congregational responsibilities. The more the church allows or even fosters this, by pandering to feminist philosophy and failing to promote the proper Biblical roles of man and woman in marriage, the more women will begin to dominate it and men fail to accept and carry out their roles.

From this it follows that a congregation which suffers from a lack of male interest or participation and leadership, ought to ask itself very seriously whether it has not failed to foster and nourish a proper relationship between men and women in marriage and in the home. If that is indeed so, and if many of the homes are ruled by domineering women, or women who do not show that self-surrendering love that the Lord requires of them, then it is not likely that such problems of the congregation will be solved until the relationship between husband and wife has first been corrected. As long as that is allowed to persist the problem is bound to show itself.

It would not be at all surprising if there is a mysterious connection between all the various imperfections and faults in marriage, and corresponding faults and problems in the church or congregation. This is not the place to spell this out, but it may not be an unrelated coincidence that the decline in growth and missionary zeal of the church coincides roughly with a time in which the mind-set of the majority of members was toward very small families or zero population growth. The fruitlessness of marriage may possibly carry over into the church or congregation.

If such things are possible, then at least one further thing follows from this, and that is the awesome responsibility and influence that women have and are bound to have in the church, not so much by taking an active part in the work of the congregation, but by being faithful, devoted and loving wives. It could well be, as has long been felt and believed, that the most powerful influence that a woman can possibly have in this world, and in the church, is as a devoted, loving wife and mother. In this role she will create a splendid marriage relationship, and a strong and loyal family, which will tend to result also in a vigorous and faithful church where men are active and accept their responsibilities with masculine determination and energy. With her paradoxical feminine power − a strength that is made perfect in weakness − she can exert far more influence and accomplish far more than she could ever do with an active involvement in the leadership and authority of the church.

For a much more thorough study of what the Word of God has to say about the role of women in the church, and the implications of women's ordination, I refer readers to my book *Earthly Images of the Heavenly Bride: the Role of Women and the Church.* [57]

Anyone who has come to understand something of this Christ/Church relationship, as lived out in marriage, will have cause to fear that the present push to have women take positions of leadership in the public worship of the congregation and to introduce women pastors and bishops into the church, will most certainly weaken and possibly ultimately destroy the church. It already seems obvious that where such practices are introduced the church is seen by men as something for women and girls, with the result that men take less and less part. Soon men will no longer go to such churches at all, for it will be seen to be unmanly. And they will be absolutely right. Such a church will bear little resemblance to the one established by Christ. It will not be the holy Bride of Christ at all, but rather part of the apostate whore which hates and persecutes the true Church of God.[58] The best thing that could happen to such a "church" is that it should destroy itself as its women bosses vie with each other and fight among themselves.

The true Church of God, on the other hand, which steadfastly resists such pressures, may find that it is hated and persecuted, just as the Lord foretold, but because it takes the Word of God seriously and remains faithful to his truth it will nevertheless survive. Though many of its faithful members may be imprisoned, and even put to death, it has the assurance of its Lord. *"Fear not little flock, for it is your Father's good pleasure to give you the kingdom."* (Luke 12:32).

---

[57] cp *Earthly Images of the Heavenly Bride: Women and the Church*, by V.S.Grieger, Luther Rose Publications, 1992

[58] cp Rev. 17

Chapter 9

OBJECTIONS
TO THE BIBLICAL MODEL

AN ANACHRONISM

Perhaps someone might say that the Christ/Church relationship could hardly have been intended as a model or archetype for marriage, certainly not from the beginning, because it is simply a fact that Christ did not come into this world till thousands of years after the creation. How could people know anything about this in those Old Testament times? And so it is an anachronism to see the Christ/Church relationship as an archetype of marriage. Marriage might rather be seen as an archetype of the relationship between Christ and his Church.

On the surface this may seem like a very devastating criticism, but in fact it fails to touch the problem at all, simply because it does not take into account the eternity of God. God is not a creature of time as we are. With him there is no past present or future in the sense that we know these elements of time. *"One day is as a thousand years, and a thousand years as one day."* (II Peter 3:8). The Bible also assures us that God knew all about us already long before we existed, in fact he chose us in Christ before the foundation of the world.[59] Once this is understood and properly taken into account, there is not the least reason why the relationship between Christ and his Church should not in fact have been the archetype for marriage. The Christ/Church relationship is an eternal one that will not cease with the end of time, but will continue for all eternity.

In this respect this is much like the Old Testament sacrifices. Every Christian knows that these sacrifices were not effective in themselves,[60] but were only types or pictures of the one great sacrifice still to come – the sacrifice of Christ on the cross. But who would suggest that because the Old Testament sacrifices preceded the sacrifice of the Lamb of God, therefore they must have been a model or archetype for the sacrifice of Christ. Not at all. It is the other way around. The great sacrifice of Christ was the original archetype which the Old Testament sacrifices were only intended to picture or illustrate. They were pointers to, or illustrations of that great sacrifice to come.

So marriage too, even though it indeed preceded the coming of Christ and the establishment of his Church, was intended as a

---

[59] cp Eph. 1:3-6

[60] cp Heb. 10:4

picture, or earthly presentation of the relationship between Christ and his Church, just as St. Paul indicates in Ephesians 5:32. If this is so, then it can be a true picture only if husband and wife pattern their lives on Christ and his Church. Just as the Old Testament saints could not change their rituals or sacrifices to suit their own ideas or preferences, without those sacrifices becoming a sacrilegious distortion of, rather than a true type of, the great sacrifice of Christ, and therefore an abomination in God's sight, so also, if marriage is a picture of the relationship between Christ and his church, man can not tamper with it to suit his own ideas or preferences, without at the same time distorting its sanctity, so that it becomes a desecration of Christ and his Church rather than a celebration. Every departure touches not only the couple and their welfare, but Christ the Lord himself. Little wonder that marriage relationships are so sensitive, so that, while a good marriage gives true joy, meaning and purpose to both partners, a bad marriage is the source of the deepest strife and distress in life, so that life becomes meaningless and empty, even though circumstances might otherwise be favourable. Marriage simply affects everything in life, work, pleasure, social life etc. When it is good, it will brighten and give joy in everything, even in the midst of poverty and pain, but when it is bad it will throw a cloud over everything so that nothing can be truly enjoyable.

SUCCESSFUL MARRIAGES OF NON-CHRISTIANS

How can non-Christians, who also get married, be guided by something they know nothing about? Moreover, there are thousands of very happy and blessed marriages among couples who know nothing at all about the Christ/Church relationship. Surely this proves that this can not be essential to a happy marriage.

This objection is really quite trivial. While we would surely all agree that it is very important that a motorist understands his car, and drives it only in accordance with the limits of its construction − if he wants to travel safely, yet nobody would say that this is contradicted by the fact that there are many motorists who really do not understand the construction of their cars or their limitations, and yet they drive safely all the time. The simple fact is that, while they may not understand how their car works, and why it does things the way it does, yet they use it and subconsciously operate within the limits of their car. Thank God that is all that is necessary to drive safely while the car is operating properly. Otherwise there would be fearful trouble. But this in no way implies that the safe driving of a car has nothing to do with operating it within the limits and purpose of its construction.

While motorists, who are quite unaware of the nature of their cars, may drive just as well as many who do know how their car is meant to operate, yet the difference comes when the car starts to give trouble. Then those who do not understand anything about how the car works are simply not in a position to get themselves out of trouble. Unless there is someone who does understand the mechanism that is giving trouble, and who can help them, they will simply not be able to travel at all. So also, many may have a fine marriage, even though they don't know how God instituted or intended it to be, if they subconsciously live out the principles that God intended for marriage. But if they find themselves in trouble, and do not know what the Creator intended, then they need help from someone who does understand.

This does not even necessarily say that Christian marriage counsellors are the only ones who can help. Just as it is possible to understand how a car operates, not only from studying the original manual of the maker, but by learning about it from experience, or from one's mates, so that one might get the car going again after it has broken down, so it is also possible for those who do not even know or recognise the Creator at all, or how he designed man and woman to live together in marriage, to learn from experience and by keeping their eyes open, how marriage should operate. But when counsellors give advice that is contrary to the intention of God the Creator and his design, this can not be of any help. Such advice is bound to destroy marriage rather than recreate and foster it. The fact that numerous non-Christians have a very happy marriage is therefore no embarrassment at all to the assertion that the Christ/Church relationship is to be the model upon which marriage is to be based. Nor does it in any way imply that man can depart from the design and intention of God in instituting marriage, or can make his own rules and principles, and that these will have just as much chance of affording true happiness. Not at all! True happiness and blessing in marriage will be attained in proportion to the degree to which the marriage followed the relationship between Christ and his Church, either consciously or unconsciously.

Obviously those who are privileged to have the Word of God — the original maker's manual, as it were — have a tremendous advantage, and if they truly want to enjoy the full blessings that God intended, they should be most happy to study this matter diligently and then to be guided by that Word. The earlier this is done in life the better, even before courtship. Before marriage the couple should make this matter a very important part of their discussions, and resolve between them that this will be their goal, so that they will help each other to attain this relationship more and more perfectly.

Until both partners are ready to make such an unconditional commitment they are not ready for marriage. But with such an understanding and serious commitment, they can look forward to the most rewarding relationship that man and woman can experience in this world. Marriage for them will be a little preview of the eternal marriage with Christ in glory. Whether they have good fortune financially or not, whether they have good health or not, whether they have many social friends or not, life will be full of meaning and interest. Such a marriage is worth more than anything else in this world. It is ultimately what God intended for us in the beginning.

TOO THEORETICAL

But someone might object that all this sounds too theoretical and idealistic. It is simply not practical in real life, where we have got to have our feet on the ground, and deal with problems from day to day as we come to them. It is the view of the writer of this book, however, that the seriousness of marriage calls for careful consideration and ideological commitment. It is simply not responsible and not good enough to drift into marriage without careful consideration and evaluation of where we are going and what we should be striving for. It is precisely this indifference – this failure to have some goal or model to imitate in our marriage, that is the cause of so much confusion and heartache later. Far from making it more difficult to attain true happiness in marriage, such a model makes it much easier and more relaxing. People who simply drift through life, now following this trend, and then that fashion, without any clear, predetermined principles are like a child who is lost in the woods. He doesn't know which way to go and what to do because he can not see far enough in front of him to tell where a particular path leads. And so he follows this path for a time, till it seems to be taking him further from home, and then he tries something else, which may turn out to be no better. What he needs is a map or diagram to indicate where all the different paths lead. Of course this is somewhat theoretical, but it is far more responsible than simply following one's whims. So also the Christ/Church relationship is a truly helpful guide to an excellent marriage.

Long before his own marriage, the author had come to see that the relationship between Christ and his Church was in fact the key to a proper, God-ordained relationship in marriage. Accordingly he chose the passage in Ephesians 5, where this is most clearly taught, as his marriage text, and endeavoured to make this the guide for his own married life. After thirty three years of practical experience, he can only say that this Christ/Church relationship was a first-class, practical help. It provided not only over-all directions as to the proper principles to be applied, but also the answer to numerous little problems and details as well. It is by far the most useful and simple guide to follow.

What about couples who have not understood the relationship between Christ and his Church as being any guide for their marriage, and have simply followed the pattern of the world about them? Is it too late for them to change course and rebuild their marriage on the foundation of the Christ/Church relationship? If they are honest with themselves they will probably have to confess that their marriage has in fact left a great deal to be desired. There have been times when they were most unhappy and sick at heart, wondering whether they might not finally split and go their separate ways. Probably their good common sense, and their sense of responsibility, forced them to hang on and try to overcome their differences, even for the sake of the children, or for the sake of their friends. But they were lacking that special experience and joy that they had so much wanted in marriage. Perhaps some have already spent time with marriage guidance counsellors being subjected to the latest techniques in psychoanalysis to determine how best to find their way through their problems.

There is only one answer. It is never too late to follow the right road or the proper path. No matter how far we might have gone down a false road, there is no point in sticking to it because we don't have the humility to go back and follow the true path. The sooner we make the decision to do so, the sooner we can enjoy the assurance that we are on the right path, and begin to rejoice in the scenery that it affords. Thank God everyone can have that assurance, not because it has been enthusiastically presented by one who has gone this road for years and found it to be most satisfying, but because we have the assurance of the Author of marriage himself that this is the right path. These are the principles on which a happy marriage is based. These are not the thoughts or principles of some man, be he psychologist, sociologist, philosopher or theologian, but they are the deliberate intention of him who designed man and woman in the first place. Man and woman were created by him in the image of God to be earthly pictures of sublime, heavenly realities, which they will not fully understand until they share in the heavenly marriage of Christ their Lord. They are privileged to carry out a special function that they do not understand; they have the honour of representing eternal mysteries, and in so doing to enjoy the most wonderful blessing and treasure in all creation − a marriage that is a picture of heaven. To turn their back on that and to reject it is ultimately to reject all meaning and purpose in life.

Chapter 10

DISTORTIONS OF MARRIAGE

DE FACTO RELATIONSHIPS

In Australia marriage is regarded not as a divine institution for life, but as little more than a contract between two people to live together as long as they consider this to be to their mutual advantage. Our laws no longer seem to frown upon unmarried people living together, but afford them the same rights and privileges as married couples. This has led to a great increase in the number of de facto couples in this country. Many probably reason that if they can enjoy the same status and privileges without being married, why should they bother? There are even some advantages in not being married. There is no need for all the legal requirements, no fee to pay, and, in case it does not work out well, there is no hassle in parting. There is no need for a divorce. They can simply go their separate ways, and that is it. And so an increasing number of couples opt for a de facto union simply because it is so easy and is not necessarily binding. If they want to get married they still have the option of doing so later.

All this is a distortion of the divine archetype or model for marriage. The main distortion is in the area of absolute commitment. While Christ and his Church are absolutely committed to each other for time and for eternity, there is no such commitment in a de facto relationship. This is the very reason for, and supposed advantage of a de facto arrangement. By its very nature it provides an easy way out, should that become desirable. Since there are no legal ties between them, which must first be dissolved, this also allows for a subsequent de facto arrangement without having to obtain legal dissolution first. It provides a paradise for irresponsible people, not able to work through and solve their difficulties, but anxious to run out on their problems. This is an affront to the clearly expressed intention of the Lord with respect to the unity of man and woman. Jesus said, *"Have ye not read, that he which made them at the beginning made them male and female, and said, For this cause shall a man leave father and mother, and shall cleave to his wife: and they twain shall be one flesh? Wherefore they are no more twain, but one flesh. What therefore God hath joined together, let not man put asunder."* (Matthew 19:4-6).

DIVORCE

In answer to the question of the Pharisees Jesus said with divine authority, *"Whosoever shall put away his wife, except it be for fornication, and shall marry another, committeth adultery: and whosoever marrieth her which is put away doth commit adultery."* (Matthew 19:9). The relationship between Christ and his Church does not change and is not terminated, even by death. It is eternal, never to be disrupted for ever and ever. For a couple, then, to disrupt their marriage and become divorced, is to use their marriage as a picture of that awful separation between Christ and those who follow Satan in hell, when Christ will say to them on the last day: *"Depart from me ye cursed into everlasting fire prepared for the devil and his angels."* (Matthew 25:41).

Surely this is the most shocking distortion of marriage, and the highest insult to its author. To abuse God and his institution of marriage in this way, by making it less than lifelong, is very serious. It desecrates the divine archetype of which marriage is intended to be a reflection, and makes it a reflection of its very opposite, not heaven but hell. This is no doubt why divorced persons suffer such fearful and horrendous consequences. As in hell nothing can possibly relieve the wicked of the bitterness and anguish of their separation from God, and every thought of him is a rebuke, so divorce does not leave the partners any peace and joy, but constantly overshadows everything they do. Every thought of their partner is loaded with torment, and every meeting adds to that torment. There is probably nothing worse that man and woman can suffer in this life than divorce. Death itself is much to be preferred. The modern trend of having divorce parties, and celebrating one's divorce, makes sense only to those who don't know what marriage is. Those who understand its true meaning can only be most deeply grieved at divorce and shocked at the thought of celebrating such a tragedy and distortion.

Jesus makes it quite clear that there is only one reason for divorce, and that is fornication.[61] This means that if the wife is guilty of fornication, the husband may procure a divorce and put her away. If the husband is guilty of fornication, the wife may obtain a divorce and separate from him. This does not mean that they are obliged to divorce their partners even in the case of fornication. Just as Christ the heavenly Bridegroom again and again forgave his unfaithful people, when they went after other gods, so the Christian couple should be ready to forgive their partner too. The reason why the church recognises divorce in the case of malicious desertion is not because desertion is a ground for divorce,

---

[61] cp Matt. 19:9

but because it is divorce in practice, albeit without a legal document. The divorce which follows malicious desertion, then, is simply a legal recognition that the other party has in fact abandoned the marriage.

What about other marriage problems that lead to a disruption of marriage? It is the belief of this writer that such difficulties are due to either one of two essential causes, or a combination of both. Some might regard this as an over simplification, but those who can think in terms of principles rather than simply incidents, will see that it is not really so. There are, according to St. Paul, two basic or essential ingredients of marriage, as we have seen. The first is that the husband loves his wife with the self-sacrificing love that Christ shows to his Church, giving himself up for her, and the second is that the wife submits herself in all things to her husband as the Church does to Christ her Lord. All the troubles which arise between married partners will show themselves in either one or the other of these two areas. Of course there are plenty of other sorts of problems in the marriage of a couple, but they do not become marriage problems or problems that threaten a marriage unless they show themselves in either of these two ways. For instance, a husband may lose his job and fail to be able to support his wife as well as they would like. This is a calamity for their married life, but it is not a marriage problem, unless the wife, because of it, refuses to subject herself to her husband and accept the burden that this places upon them. A wife may suffer from some disability that prevents her from doing her duty in some respect. This is indeed a handicap, but does not become a marriage problem unless the husband fails to show that self-sacrificing love for her that understands her problem and accepts her for what she is.

Unless all such things are remedied reasonably quickly, they not only grow, but beget further troubles as a reaction from the partner. The solution is not divorce. That is simply legalising the problem and giving it permanency. Christ assures us that there is only one cause for divorce and that is fornication.[62] Other difficulties can be cured if the parties are willing to swallow their pride, and return to the principles outlined throughout this book.

Unfortunately a great many people, faced with such matters, are simply not willing to accept the biblical solution. They claim what is called "irretrievable breakdown", and proceed to seek a divorce, in the hope that they may have better luck with someone else next time round. But what does this say? For one thing it surely says that unless they have undergone a drastic change of

---

[62] cp Matt. 19:9

heart and mind they will not be fit for a second marriage. They are almost bound to have a repeat of the same problem. Statistics show that this is the case. The chances of a successful second marriage for divorcees is far less than for their first marriage. The writer of this book is not usually too interested in statistics, because they only show us what we should have expected if we properly understood the principles of conduct involved. It is such principles that determine statistics, not the other way around. Statistics should not determine principles. In other words we should learn how to behave from sound principles, not from statistics. However, when people refuse to listen to sound principles, statistics may sometimes demonstrate that they had better take notice of proper principles.

But why should the second marriage of a divorced person be so much more prone to disaster? Anyone who has come to see that there are two basic causes of marriage problems will have no trouble in understanding the reason for this. Let us suppose that, for some reason, the husband in the first marriage cared more for himself and his own interests than for his wife. When she did commit herself to him, her trust was betrayed and she was only hurt by him. She can possibly point to numerous occasions in which her self-surrender was thus rewarded only by insult and abuse. How will this affect her? Obviously she is not going to continue to be used and abused by such a callous lack of love and understanding, and so she refuses to give herself fully to her partner. She believes her experience teaches her that it is too dangerous to commit herself fully to a man. He will only take advantage of her to her deep wounding and hurt. If she is divorced she will have been through a great many such heart-breaking experiences, and may well have become hardened into refusing to commit herself fully to her husband.

What will happen then if she should enter upon a second marriage? The chances are pretty high that, while she may initially hope that her new husband is much more understanding and loving than her ex-husband, otherwise she would not be interested in marrying him, yet she believes that experience has taught her that it is too risky to commit herself fully and unconditionally to a man. She must play safe lest she fall prey to the same abuse and insults that led to the destruction of her first marriage. Once bitten she is twice shy. She may therefore refuse to give herself fully and unconditionally to her new husband, and insist upon a good measure of independence and self-determination. But this is a recipe for disaster. The very way in which she seeks to protect herself will quickly become the means by which she destroys her chances of a happy union. Unless a wife commits herself absolutely and unconditionally to her husband, he will not long be able to show that self-sacrificing love for her that is so necessary for their welfare. And so the cycle will begin over again. Disaster is at the door because she learned her lesson wrongly.

If a couple can not solve their problems, but seek divorce as a way out, they are on very dangerous ground for any second marriage. What they need to do is to be guided not by their previous experiences, as they think, but by him who instituted marriage, and knows exactly what is required.

What has been said here in connection with divorce and second marriage should not be taken to imply that the author is in any way favourable toward divorce, as a way of avoiding matrimonial disaster. On the contrary, he is committed to the teaching of Christ that fornication is the only biblical ground for divorce. And even that need not necessarily result in divorce. All divorce, by its very nature, quite apart from the circumstances, is a tragedy, in that it distorts the divine archetype of marriage to dishonour Christ. A senior pastor, whose marriage was far from ideal, said on one occasion, "A bad marriage is better than a good divorce." But there is no reason why humble children of God, who are ready to learn from their Lord, should not be able to overcome their difficulties and have a good and most glorious marriage.

HOMOSEXUALITY

No doubt the worst travesty of marriage, as a picture of the heavenly archetype, is homosexuality, whatever its causes. Homosexuality is often what might be called a second generation distortion of marriage. That is to say it is the result of conditioning from previous marriage problems. Those causes may sometimes seem relatively innocent and respectable, but the result is an utter desecration of marriage.

It sometimes happens that a couple come into difficulties in their marriage, so that they fail to communicate meaningfully. The wife may nag her husband and try to get him to pull his weight in the home, but he can't take the nagging from his wife, and so prefers to keep out of her way. He seeks peace by abdicating from his position as the head of the house, and puts in his time with other friends or workmates. Instead of solving the problem together, according to the principles of the Christ/Church relationship, the couple resign themselves to living with it as best they can, at least for the time being, in the hope that the problem might just go away later. In any case divorce is hardly an option at this stage because they have a number of young children to whom they are committed. The wife might decide to ignore her husband while he is around the house, and devote herself to the children so that at least they will turn out all right.

But the question is, will they turn out all right? Children who are reared in the environment of a dominant mother and weak-kneed father, who keeps out of the way as much as possible, have a very poor chance of getting their values and priorities straight. Little boys in the family need a dominant father image to develop or at least to refine their masculinity. Of course they will be males, whether they like it or not, but they may well fail to develop the proper masculine traits of initiative and leadership. Having little respect for a father who largely ignores them and their mother, they may well lose respect also for their own sex. They are too young to appreciate the economic role still perhaps provided by their father in supporting the family. All they know is that he is away from home and doesn't seem to care or contribute much to the family. Such boys, who are left little choice but to identify more closely with their mother, may begin to develop feminine qualities. In this way the stage is being set for homosexual characteristics. The lack of a proper father image and a dominant mother may completely undermine their identity and leave them confused. If their attitude is not corrected before they grow up, such young males will often either become homosexuals or find a girl who will dominate them. By their lack of masculine leadership and initiative, they will soon create the conditions that lead their wives to have to take the reins and run the household. Thus the condition becomes self-perpetuating. The next generation will face the same problem, possibly with even more aggravation. The only end to that road is homosexuality, and the road must end only because homosexual relationships are sterile and barren. This was undoubtedly the design of the Creator because such relationships are unfit for the rearing of children.

Not only are little boys affected by such reversed roles in the marriage of their parents, but also little girls can be greatly damaged. They too need a sound father-image, someone who can handle them firmly and love them powerfully. Where this is lacking they will feel rejected and unloved. They will grow up with a disrespect or even resentment for their father, and this may well be transferred to men in general, most probably also to their husband, if they ever marry. The leadership and capacity of their mother to run the household, and in fact everything, for all they know, may well conjure up in their minds an image of woman as the dominant, and in fact only worthwhile partner. Despising men and seeing women as the aggressive, initiating sex, the stage is set for a grand repeat of the problem in their own marriage. They may insist on being boss and wearing the pants in their own

89

marriage, so that they will find for themselves a man who is weak enough or unprincipled enough to allow this. Again the problem becomes self-perpetuating. It is not surprising that the end of this road too may well be lesbianism and a hatred for all men. Happily there is no deeper degeneration possible for genetic reasons. This is the bottom of the pit. For homosexuals to marry and to adopt children, or even to mother children by artificial insemination, is a prostitution not only of marriage, but also of motherhood, made possible only by a scientific miscarriage.

Some evidence seems to suggest that homosexual propensity may be innate so that children can be born with homosexual preferences, rather than this develop later from their environment. The Christian knows, of course, that we all have a propensity for every kind of evil by birth, because of our sinful nature.[63] Certainly this includes a propensity for every kind of sexual evil. If there is a marked, innate, homosexual propensity due to hormonal imbalance this could also be due to a condition of the mother which prepares the ground for such a hormonal imbalance. Every evil seems to have the unfortunate tendency to self-perpetuation.[64]

---

[63] cp Gen 6:5; 8:21; Job 14:4; Jer. 17:9; John 3:6
[64] cp John 3:6

Chapter 11

GLORIOUS FULFILMENT
FOR MAN AND WOMAN

In as much as couples attempt to follow the Christ/Church relationship in their marriage, they will find the greatest joy and
satisfaction that is possible for them here in this world. It will be
a beautiful foretaste of heaven and a salutary preparation for it.
Of course, the fact that we are sinners, and that we fail to do the
will of God even though we may desperately want to, will mean
that our marriage will never truly imitate the glorious relationship between Christ and his Church. We are simply not capable
of such perfection. But the point is that it is only to the extent
that we are successful in following that direction that our marriage will be truly rewarding.

After all this has been said, many people may still be concerned
with the modern belief that woman is in a position of inferiority
with respect to man. The very terms "head" and "subjection" immediately conjure up a distasteful feeling of the wife being put
down and denigrated by a domineering tyrant of a husband. The
very idea of submission seems to be degrading. Such a feeling is
understandable in our present age, surrounded as we are by people who know of, and can think of greatness and glory, only in
terms of physical power and strength. But such people are to be
pitied, and hopefully enlightened. They have lost touch with some
of the finer and more subtle realities of life. Nevertheless they
are without excuse, for there are still many evidences of greatness
and glory in feminine subjection and submission, which are obvious to everyone, also in some of the more noble things in life. Any-
body who appreciates traditional ballroom dancing or figure
skating must surely be impressed by this. What is the relationship between man and woman in these activities? Obviously it is
man who is the initiator, the leader, and the enabler, and woman
who is the responder, the follower who submits to his leadership.
But who is it that has the real glory in this exercise? Is it the man
just because he is the leader? Not if we have our eyes open. Headship and leadership are not in themselves recipients of glory. It
is the woman's part – she who is led and who follows – to have
the glory. All eyes are on her most of the time, the man's movements are appreciated only because of what they enable her to do.
Everything is designed to make the most of her – her dress, her
figure, her agility, her feminine grace and charm. She is the cen-

tre of attraction, and yet it is in her response and her commitment to her partner that she is presented in her greatest glory. She is the one who gets the greatest applause, and she is the one who receives the flowers when the performance is over. Everything that happens gives glory to her.

Does this make the male partner envious of her? Not at all. That is the way he wants it to be. He may, perhaps, even have done the hardest feats, lifting his partner above his head and balancing her with one hand and so on, things that she could not do for him. But she receives the flowers, and he applauds her without envy. What is his reward? Simply the honour of being her partner and the privilege of dancing or skating with her in such a way that she is glorified. And why is that so deeply satisfying to him? Because the whole performance was an enactment of the proper relationship between man and woman. By allowing him to be her head and leader she is most honoured, and by exulting her he too is glorified. That is how it was intended to be – that is how it ought to be. This is just exactly as St. Paul presents it in that passage in Ephesians. The headship of man is in no way denigrating to woman. It is intended for her greatest glory and honour.

Perhaps we ought to ask ourselves also, why it is that women generally love weddings? Everybody knows that women enjoy weddings far more than men do. Right from childhood, as little girls they were already playing at weddings. Their own wedding is considered the very climax of their life – their ultimate glory. And yet it is at their wedding that they traditionally bind themselves to a man for life, for better or for worse. Is that really so wonderful? Not according to much popular thinking. "Oh!", some will say, "It's not the occasion that makes it so good. It is the dress. Girls like wearing pretty dresses, you see." But wait a minute. Isn't it possible for them to wear even more beautiful dresses on other occasions? How come, then, that it is the bridal dress which is really seen as marking the climax or peak of glory in a woman's life? Simply because, as wiser and more understanding generations before our time knew very well, for a woman to become a bride – committed to a man, is the most significant thing in her life. It is the achievement in a life-time, that by which she finds true fulfilment to be what she was designed to be. It is in marriage that she is brought to her true glory. And that innate conviction has not yet been completely destroyed. Deep down in the heart of every woman, unless it has been cruelly suppressed, by brainwashing through the media, or by bitter abuse in life, is a deep feeling and conviction that she really does not want to be the head, with all the responsibility and self-sacrifice that that involves. She is designed, with all her feminine grace and charm, to be the glory of man. That is her role in which she will shine and excel. Therefore she wants to marry a real man, who takes the initiative, who is a leader that commands respect, someone who is strong and determined, ready to stand for his convictions, who is not afraid to suffer, and who is motivated by a self-sacrificing love to make her his own, who will adore her, admire her, sustain her, lift her up to her greatest heights as his glorious queen. This is the most satisfying and rewarding life for both man and woman. It gives honour to man and glory to woman.

Lord, who at Cana's wedding feast
  Didst as a guest appear,
Thou dearer far than earthly guest,
  Vouchsafe Thy presence here;
For holy Thou indeed dost prove
  The marriage vow to be,
Proclaiming it a type of love
  Between the Church and Thee

On those who at Thine altar kneel,
  O Lord, Thy blessing pour,
That each may wake the other's zeal
  To love Thee more and more.
O grant them here in peace to live,
  In purity and love,
And, this world leaving, to receive
  A crown of life above.

Adelaide Thrupp
1853

Feminist View

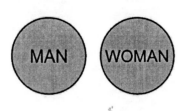

Individuals
*Man and woman are
equal competitors*

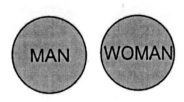

Marriage
*A legal contract between
two independent individuals.
A 50/50 relationship with
equal authority*

Society *Men and women in equal competition with each other,
having interchangeable roles and equal rights and responsibilities.
Unisex patterns tending to erase masculine and feminine qualities*

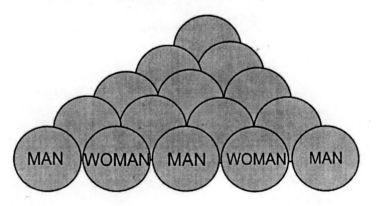

Christian View

Individuals
Man and woman are
complementary counterparts

Marriage
A mutually dependent unit (one
flesh) for life.
The husband as head of the wife,
and the wife as the glory of man

Society
Men and women in
partnership with each
other, having
complementary roles
and interests. Both
equal in worth and
importance;
emphasising and
appreciating their
masculine and feminine
qualities

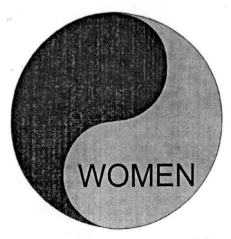

Any similarity between this illustration and the Chinese yin and yang symbols
is purely incidental, and indicates no affinity whatsoever.

CPSIA information can be obtained at www.ICGtesting.com
Printed in the USA
BVOW02s2157281214

381058BV00010B/231/P